Happy Birthd a

From— Vernon and Irma Grundman

Dedicated to those who
remember the "little house out back."

———————■———————

MY FOLKS
BACK TO THE BASICS:
A Treasury Of Outhouse Stories

Capper Press
Topeka, Kansas

Editor, Lay-Out and Production Coordinator:
Michele R. Webb

Contributing Editor:
Sheri R. Daudet

Illustrator:
Stephen B. Falls

ISBN: 0-941678-41-5

FOREWORD

Although the subject of the "little house out back," known better as the outhouse, is a delicate one, it is a topic that has generated so much interest that we have documented some of our readers' "outhouse experiences." This is meant to be a fun, lighthearted, and tasteful book, and is in no way meant to offend the sensibilities of our readers.

Our purpose for this nostalgic addition to the dynamic *My Folks* series is to document the trials and tribulations of, adventures in, and affection for, the outhouse, a rare sight in this time of technology and indoor plumbing. It was a vital component of the working household of its era, and has also provided many topics of conversation and great tales handed down from one generation, now to the next.

Aside from its obvious purpose, many folks saw the outhouse as a place for retreat, and even as a meeting place, that brings back special memories of family, friends, and home. Our hope is that those who have never had the "privy-lege" (to quote contributor Della Bledsoe) of using the "outdoor convenience" will better understand the unique place the outhouse holds in the hearts of many after reading the authors' perspectives.

We make no claim of complete historical accuracy, but offer these letters as personal glimpses into the past as it is remembered by those who lived it. I have, in an attempt to maintain the authentic flavor of the letters, made few spelling, punctuation or grammatical corrections.

We thank and salute our contributors, who made it possible to share this book with a new generation of readers.

Michele Webb
Editor

CONTENTS

CHAPTER 1: The Little Houses of Yore

The Outhouse

If you have never used a modern day outhouse, in those days you might be surprised how very efficient they were for relief, economy, and comfort to some extent. Generally speaking they were approximately six by seven feet and eight feet to the roof. The high-classed ones were sided with tongue and groove siding and placed over a deep pit, the deeper the better. It was a pretty good idea to take a good breath of air just before you went in and to exhale quickly when you went out, because the staunch odor didn't smell exactly like a rose. Over the pit was a seat that usually extended the length of the outhouse. There could be one to three holes on it cut to fit the different sizes. The smallest was made to fit the littlest fellow and to keep him intact.

It always seemed that there was plenty of ventilation from the cracks, especially in the winter time when a freezing wind whistled up from below. Some of the uptown outhouses had a crescent-shaped moon cut out near the top, maybe more for decoration than for ventilation. Leading to the outhouse was a well-worn path that was traveled out by the runner with far greater speed than his or her return to the house.

No Montgomery Ward catalogues were ever thrown away. They were saved to be hung on the wall closest to the big hole.

Marie Swisher
Coldwater, Kansas

Down The Little Board Path

You certainly can't eliminate from history that homely object, "The Privy." If you've never had the "privy-lege" of using one, you can understand their importance by simply going out on a camping trip, sans (without) porta-potty! If nature abuses you with a spell of summer complaint and you are out there under a big bushy tree and suddenly a sudden unexpected downpour occurs, that's the height of adding insult to injury. Then the vision of the little grey board shed with a new moon cut out in the gable is second to none in miracles.

Those of us who grew up familiar with outdoor toilets will never take for granted such an item as bathroom tissue. Not if your memory of the Sears or Wards catalogue remains with you. As soon as the new book arrived at the mailbox, the old issue was promptly taken to the toilet. It was hung across a wire or cord - handy to reach.

By this time all the pages left in the old book were the smooth glossy ones, so we girls, anticipating the fact that the new book would soon be in like condition, would tear out some of the very thin pages and fold them into tiny squares and secret them in under the shingles, or in a glass jar and hide them out under the shrubbery or under the floor for later use. All that yack about corn cobs? Well, newly-shelled corn cobs are soft and feathery and sanitary and better by far than a glossy page of a catalogue with colored dye to consider.

Not all things about the old building was bad. If you sat quietly you could hear the wren's babies cheep in their nesting box fastened on the outside wall, and with a little luck the breeze blew from the right direction to overwhelm the room with odors of lilac and honeysuckle.

At any rate, thinking about all this makes me smile....I hope you'll join me!

Della Bledsoe
Oceanside, California

Little Houses Of Yore

The traditional outhouse was usually at the end of a well-worn path leading to a hidden spot in the grove.

Hollyhocks or a climbing vine secluded the little facility. If it was an elite outhouse the walls might be covered with left-over wallpaper.

Occasionally a mail order catalog was laid between the seats - for reading, of course.

One of the assets was that it provided a hideaway for the kids when dishes were to be done.

The outhouses provided refuge for spiders, bees, crickets, or an occasional lizard.

Winter time provided a far different story. Snow blew in through the cracks around the door and windows, so a quick brush off was necessary before taking a seat.

The floor and seats got a real good scrubbing every week. When the hot, soapy water from the wringer washing machine was drained, it was carried to use for scrubbing.

Ah — those were the days! If one wanted solitude, that was the place to find it.

Madonna Storla
Postville, Iowa

"House of Many Styles"

I told my grandchildren that I was looking forward to reading about outhouses. They think one would be great and want me to tell all about them.

I described the outhouse as having been built in many different styles. Early American, Dutch, French Provincial, and Spanish. They were generally placed where the wind could hit them from all sides. Occasionally they were placed under a shade tree. We lived one place where it was tacked on to the far side of the chicken house. I think I will skip over the bad things, such as flies, wasps and snakes.

The good things I remember are:
1) The speed with which it served its customers. No one ever had

to stand in line. Extreme cold or sweltering heat hurried them along.

2) They were very economical, one sack of lime each spring was the total expense. During the Depression this was a great help.

3) Country schools that could afford toilet tissue got a 3A rating in my book.

4) They furnished a lot of entertainment for the young people on Halloween each fall.

Maybe you young ones of today have missed a few things after all.

Rebecca Swafford
Savannah, Missouri

Lesson Never Forgotten

Outhouses — what memories are conjured up with the mention of that word — memories instilled in our youthful minds as our grandmother related the settling of a pioneer homestead, upon which the outhouse played such an important part. Bleached by the relentless summer sun, or penetrated by winter blasts, it served an additional purpose in giving a feeling of "getting settled" to the pioneer family.

Growing up on the farm in the era preceding the installation of running water in most homes, we have a great many memories and experiences connected with outhouses.

We oftentimes heard people referring to their outhouses as "one," "two," or "three holers," and our childish minds judged their financial status accordingly.

Occasionally we youngsters used this little building "out back" not only for comfort's sake, but to hide in as we played "Hide and Seek" or to delay beginning washing the dishes. At times, we sought to evade our turn to fill the wood box. I clearly remember my attempt to escape a well-deserved chastisement by locking myself in the outhouse until I hoped my mother's disapproval had abated, only to find my reward waiting for me. It was a lesson I never forgot.

The inside walls of some outhouses became bulletin boards to proclaim the names of a certain romantic duo, or the name or initials of the latest "heart throb." The names of salesmen or their company phone numbers, names of new brands of seed or oil, or other farm memos might appear on these walls, as the farmer jotted them as he worked around the farm yard and lacked paper to write on at the moment.

Today I am thankful for my modern bathroom with its wide mirrors, colorful porcelain fixtures and shiny chrome, but I am glad to have experienced the days of the outhouse, as it has helped me to really appreciate what we have now.

Reva M. Smith
Abilene, Kansas

"Sweet" Memories

A friend's description of her family's outhouse in mid-Minnesota, some 60 years ago, proved very interesting.

A lengthy pathway in natural stone led to the little house, she said, a joy in summer, but extra long in winter. Dense vines of pink and lavendar flowers climbed the trellis at its entrance, with no need of closing the door. She remembers the hum of bees and fragrance of peach and plum trees that grew close by. It was a good place to be alone and meditate, she added. Paneled wainscotting lined the bottom of the "fancy" outhouse, with blue walls above. It was her job, she said, to make a new curtain, when needed, for the one window. There were three holes, small, medium and large.

Tissue-like wrappings from peaches and other boxed fruit were saved from canning season. These were neatly flattened by the children and pushed onto a spindle (a large nail hammered thru a board from beneath).

Once a year, a man was hired to topple the house, and clean it out. There was a $10 fee, quite a little for that time. When the job was finished, lye was added, and sometimes ashes, to keep it "sweet."

Marjorie Lundell
Casa Grande, Arizona

From Outhouse to Outhouse

Outhouses? What lady discusses outhouses? Oh well, my first experience, other than the novely of visiting, was our move to a country home where the big white house had an accompanying little white house with its graduated holes, the smallest one about 14" from the well-scrubbed wood floor. The flat stone walk to it led behind shrubs and bushes.

Although the door, with its cut out slim moon, was not facing any regular traffic, it was still concealed behind a five foot fence. The interior was cozy, the walls sealed and papered with leftover house paper. It had two small, shuttered windows, the lime bucket and dipper in the corner, and the catalogue hung on the wall. Of course each accommodation had its own hinged lid, which should be closed before leaving; also pull the door "almost closed." Each week the seats and floor were scrubbed with rinse water from the clothes washing

Later, to modernize, the beloved little w.h. was replaced with the cement version made by the W.P.A. Now there was roll tissue. No more interesting reading!

After many years of modern bathrooms, I had an interesting experience at a "Johnny On The Spot." The "Privey" areas were well-marked to a secluded area behind a board fence. As I was starting to enter, some men were leaving. When I asked for the women's area they just pointed to where they had come! At 75, I was ready for a new experience, I guess. From outhouse to outhouse in one exciting lifetime. Modern, no catalogue.

Kathryn Jackson
Eureka, Kansas

Proud of Modern Facility

My mother took such pride in keeping our outhouse pretty. She insisted Daddy put her in a window and she kept fresh curtains up. There was a "wishbook" for us to look at by day and a flashlight handy to keep us from being scared of the dark. Mama kept a fresh coat of paint on the walls, a "modern" seat on it for our comfort and lime for us to sprinkle to keep odors down.

After I married and went home for visits, Mama had even installed an electric light. We still tease her about always having the most "modern" outhouse in her neighborhood.

Jean Hardy
Perryton, Texas

Outhouses I and II

The Outhouse, variously dubbed "Private," "White" or "Red," (depending on the color) was the source of protection from dishwashing, floor scrubbing, and/or punishment.

Number one was the home outhouse. Last year's Montgomery Ward or Sears catalogue afforded hours of browsing entertainment. The usefulness was evident by the absence of the black and white softer sheets, leaving only the heavier colored pages to read. Two catalogues put one in the "rich" class.

Number two was the outhouse at school. It was, of course, much larger with a single door in the high board fence in front, and no doors at the openings to the stalls. As I remember, there were five stalls, with a catalogue in each. We were lined up outside and allowed five in at a time. Teachers took turns at supervising, as at playground duty. On cold days, depending on the wind and the number needing to "go," we were sometimes packed inside the fence for protection. At other times, we were kept inside and the allotted number sent from the cloakroom. There was, I suppose, a duplicate for the boys.

Dorothy Jacobs
Felt, Oklahoma

Escaping the Hum Drum

At school many times, the hum-drum of study sessions became somewhat boring. One grew weary of tracing Civil War battles, or of extracting the square root of six-digit numbers, or of diagramming "mile-long" sentences, etc. This was an ideal time to fake the necessity of going to the privey. By eyeing the improvised "signal board" at the back of the room, one knew the "coast was clear" when the white side, instead of the black one, was in view (showing that someone else was out of the room at that time). This was the time to hold your hand high with two fingers up, which meant, "May I go?" If the teacher's eye seemed to evade you, you could shake your hand more vigorously so she would assume an emergency existed and would likely nod consent. You then hurriedly turned the signal board and rushed through the door.

Daisy Brown
Prairie Village, Kansas

Moving On Up

Our outhouse was a special one. Most all the neighbors around our farm had just got bathrooms in their house, but we couldn't do that so I remember the special work Dad put inside our "outside bathroom." Freshly-painted walls with padded covers to set on with lift-up covers for our eight brothers who had poor aim.

An extension cord was strung through the kitchen window for lights and a portable heater, so when we'd get up in the morning Dad would plug the lights and heater in for us. We really thought that was moving up in the world.

Name Withheld
Minnesota

Witty Wallpaper

How well I remember the old outhouse back in Kansas! In good weather we tolerated it, in winter we hated it. But ours was different. It was during World War II. My sister and I and our girlfriends were in our teens. We just had to do something to improve that little house out back. We cut jokes from magazines or wherever we could find them. Then taking paste, we pasted those jokes on the inside walls until they were covered!

Mrs. Lawrence Stoddard
Hereford, Texas

Double-Decker

The strangest outhouse I ever saw was a newspaper picture of one in Massachusetts. It was a two-story one, attached to the house. From the upper floor one would walk to the far end to sit down. There was a partition between the upper and lower floors. Persons entering from the downstairs went to the near side. It must have been very nice not to have to shovel a path through the snow to the back of the lot in the wintertime!

Mildred White
Richfield, Utah

Culture Shock

I once went to work in a developing country (Kenya). There the floor of the outhouse is made of a slab of concrete or a platform of planks with a hole about 6 x 8 inches in the middle. The trick is to get into position to hit that hole. It is a hit and miss procedure.

The most unusual toilet I ever saw was in the Castle of Chillon. There was a little windowseat-like shelf in the corner of the room. When the guide lifted the lid, there was the round hole and you could look — it seemed like hundreds of miles — down into Lake Geneva. How could anyone relax and accomplish anything on a place like that?

Wilma Gill
Orlando, Florida

Uptown With The W.P.A.

Under President Roosevelt, the W.P.A. put men to work building toilets. They were constructed with cement bases to be more sanitary and they had lids. This was for safety, too. The door had to be closed at all times to keep out toddlers that were unattended and might fall in.

With this new outhouse we really thought we were living uptown.

Dorothy Rohlfs
Seward, Nebraska

Next?

Forty-five years ago our neighbors had an unusual outhouse. One whole side of the woodshed was partitioned off for it. There were four hand-carved holes and each had a hand-made cover. On one cover was lettered: "You are next."

There was a window at the far end, and a candle and matches and reading material on the shelf. Within easy reach was the Sears Roebuck and Montgomery Ward catalogs to be used for "tissue."

Irma Thicke
LaCrescent, Minnesota

Pretty Project

About 1936 our family moved from Chicago to a small town in central Illinois where we were introduced to the "outhouse." Ours was a classic - cold, drab and drafty.

It was while Mother was still unpacking boxes that my oldest sister decided to make the outhouse her "project."

As Mother would empty a box, we were sent to fetch it out back to the work area. There my sister would cut open each box, lay it flat and measure out sheets of cardboard to fit and line the inner walls and door of the outhouse.

All this activity soon caught the attention of the local kids and they were having a high old time laughing at the "city brats" hard at work on the outhouse.

By using the unprinted side, Big Sis had a perfectly clean work surface - an ideal place to create a "work of art."

Armed with pencil, poster-paint, brushes and imagination, her outhouse "mural" took the form of an underwater seascape.

Now the neighbor kids were watching with rapt attention as my sister started to draw all manner of exotic fish, seaweed, bubbles, coral and even a friendly sort of octopus. By the time she was ready to do the painting, my sister's project had become a neighborhood effort, and every kid on the block wanted to join in the fun.

Oh, the benefits we reaped from that funny outhouse were endless. We made friends that day. Later in the fall, ours was the only outhouse left standing the morning after Halloween.

And...when winter came the cardboard acted as insulation and kept our top sides fairly warm. Of course our bare bottoms were still exposed to the elements, but somehow that "work of art" managed to see us thru till indoor plumbing came to town.

Roberta Farrell
Gatewood, Missouri

Piano-Box Privy

My husband's folks came from Missouri to the Panhandle of Oklahoma on the railroad, bringing their furniture, cattle, mules, chickens, etc. in a box car. Their piano was put in a hand-made box, and that box was used for their "outhouse" for a few years till they had money to build a better one, and then it was used as a hen coop.

Mrs. Sammie Matter
Hooker, Oklahoma

Rooftop Roosters

My first year of teaching school in 1927 provided many not-so-pleasant experiences in the little house out back.

The little house had no roof. When it snowed, the snow had to be brushed away before sitting down. It was definitely no reading room as the most disconcerting fact that the turkeys roosted around the top. No one had trained them to face the outside world when roosting!

Maude L. Butler
Brighton, Colorado

Dining Chair Extraordinaire

About a month ago we began tearing our old house down to build a new one. We had to have an outhouse. We dug the hole one afternoon. My husband and a friend were going to work on it while I went shopping for groceries.

When I returned an hour later they had it built! What a house! It was framed of 2 x 4s with paneling for walls on three sides, no door at all. But the seat was the laughing matter. They had cut a hole in a wooden dining chair and placed it over the hole.

It works, but I laugh every time I use it. Oh yes, a sheet of metal for a roof.

Shirley Duchett
Mill Spring, Missouri

Paying for the Privy

While I was raising my family of five boys and one girl, we still had to use the little house out back. One of the kids had heard about the pay restrooms for the public, and even tho our little outhouse was very rugged, they took a pork and bean can and nailed it on the outside of the door and put a sign by it — 10¢. To their surprise one day after an uncle had visited, they found a dime in their can.

Name Withheld
Missouri

Flag Posted For Privacy

The best thing about Grandma's outhouse was the red metal flag like the one on rural mailboxes. My mother explained that when Grandma's rather large family was growing up they used to put the flag down before they went in, and put it back up when they came out. This was to show when the outhouse was in use and prevent any invasion of privacy. Of course at my age I didn't have much privacy so the idea of the red flag was very appealing, and I used it every time. Once, I recall, I became too interested in looking at the pictures on the bathroom tissue (an old mail order catalog) and was absent so long that my mother came looking for me. I became upset because she had opened the door on me when the red flag was down and had invaded my privacy.

Then, one Sunday afternoon in late summer, Grandpa had something to show us. It was some rattles from a rattlesnake he had killed a few days earlier. That was enough to make my hair stand on end, but then my dad asked where he had killed it. Of all places, Grandpa said it had been in front of the outhouse! In that one awful moment my infatuation with the outhouse was gone forever. After that I set the world speed record going to and from the outhouse, and I didn't even stop to put the red flag down.

Penny M. Smith
Oberlin, Kansas

Paper Caper

It was 1936 and my father had just received a government bonus for his World War I service. Payment was made in $50 bonds. Using one of those bonds, our family of four spent ten days traveling through parts of Missouri, Arkansas, Texas (clear to the gulf), Oklahoma and back to Kansas.

While traveling in western Arkansas, we stopped out in the country at a filling station which had a little old outhouse out back. Being a "city girl," I found this place to be very interesting. During the few minutes I tarried there, I read a verse someone had carefully written on the wall, almost like a note telling later occupants why the writer happened to be there. Now this subject is a rather touchy one to write about, requiring carefully-chosen words so as to not offend. The verse was immediately "etched" into my memory. Here it is:

"Someone's pulled an awful caper,
Left me here without any paper.
The flat's all fixed
And I can't linger, "_____
(And the last two lines were a real humdinger!)

Most memories of that trip have long-ago faded away, but sorry to say, I remember that WHOLE verse better than I remember any of the beautiful poetry we had to learn in school!

Christine A. Scott
Newton, Kansas

Grandpa Rose To The Occasion

We live a mile from town and were getting ready to celebrate our fiftieth anniversary. Our four children and their spouses, our twelve grandchildren and six great-grandchildren were to be here for a week to ten days, and our two bathrooms would hardly be sufficient, especially with our poor septic tank.

But Grandpa rose to the occasion. He bought plywood and built an outhouse. I insisted he paint it brown so that it wouldn't stand out too much. The inside, however, was left light and inspired the kids to make up humorous verses and sign their names. Those walls make interesting reading.

For more comfort in the outhouse, Grandpa put an old bathroom stool seat on one of the two holes. When visiting this special toilet one little city boy took one look at the seat and said, "It won't work! It won't flush!"

Blanche Collins
Sun City, Kansas

Neighborly Advice

The little outhouse was a very important building in years past. The pretty calendars found their way to decorate the wall when the year ran out.

A friend asked his neighbor where could he buy toilet tissue. The neighbor told him to look in the index of his Montgomery Ward catalog. The friend said, "If I had a Montgomery Ward catalog, I wouldn't need to buy toilet tissue!"

Mrs. Robert Colville
King City, Missouri

Word Spread Far and Wide

I have many memories of our outhouse in northern Minnesota. Unlike many outhouses in our small town, ours was very well built. I know because my father built it and I watched him. After digging the pit, he dug four holes for the corner posts, long cedar logs around which he poured cement. Father was a mason and liked to pour concrete, which he hand-mixed in a large homemade trough.

Father was also a pretty good carpenter. After the cement was set he built the outhouse using sturdy lumber and anchoring it firmly to the corner posts. Our outhouse was solid, might as well have been made of brick. Of course, Father had good reason for building it as he did.

In those days outhouses were fair game for Halloween pranksters who delighted in tipping them over. Those poorly built or anchored were often overturned, the work of some gang of husky youngsters.

Most of the kids in our neighborhood had watched my father build our outhouse. The word was spread far and wide, and nobody ever attempted a tipover.

A.F. Rausell
Rio Rancho, New Mexico

Paint The Town Red

Even tho our little outhouse was very primitive, we all took pride in fixing it up real comfortable and bright, right down to the Sears and Roebuck catalogue. One day the kids decided the seat needed painting. All the paint they could find was bright red enamel, so they painted it all real nice and left it to dry. But long before it began to dry, company came. Them little boys' eyes sure got big when they saw the company (a large heavy-set woman and a daughter) go into the little outhouse. They hid and waited for them to come out, then they hurried in to see if any of the pretty red enamel was left on the seat.

Name Withheld
Missouri

Father Complained of Cold

I was ten years old when we moved to a place that had, miracles of miracles, running water and an indoor bathroom. I thought it was wonderful. My dad grumbled and complained because the plastic toilet seat was too <u>cold</u>.

Allie Hitz
Rainier, Oregon

Fit For A Queen

My memory of the outhouse is using great-grandma's cape. My mother kept the cape hanging in a corner of the kitchen, to be used by all members of our family for our trips to the outhouse.

Great-grandma's cape was a heavy plush fabric with heavy lining with a large hook and eye at the neckline. It was so warm to wear on the walk to the outhouse, but what I remember most is that it draped around my body completely, making me snuggly warm as a queen on her throne.

Mrs. Fred H.F. Duin
George, Iowa

The Main Attraction

Some years ago we had a party and supper for the coach and conference girls' basketball team. While the girls were enjoying the games, one girl asked where to find the bathroom. When we explained we only had "a little house out back," all the girls wanted to go see it, for they all had bathroom facilities at their homes.

They all giggled and thought it was great to set on those holes. One girl had her camera with her so she took pictures of some of the girls sitting on the holes.

The little house brought more ohs and ahs and more laughter than any of the other party games.

Minnie Mauman
Craig, Missouri

Winter Wonderland

It had started snowing at bedtime the night before. How excited I was, for in our valley we only had snow once every few years and I loved snow. To me it was one of God's miracles. I awakened next morning as Dad was preparing to go to work. As I sat up I noticed someone had taken the pot, which we kept in the bedroom for night use, out. I remembered last night's snow and wanted to see if it was still there, so I decided I needed to use the outhouse. Ordinarily, I was very much afraid of the dark, but I pulled on my boots, put a coat over my pajamas and stepped outside.

Everything was covered with a 6-inch mantle of white. To this eleven-year-old it looked like a fairyland. All fear of night vanished. I walked slowly to the outhouse, visited it and walked slowly back to the house, savoring every moment of this magical world. In daylight it was beautiful, but the magical touch was gone.

As I look back now I am thankful we did not have indoor plumbing, otherwise I never would have been allowed out in the dark and would have missed this wonderland memory.

Mrs. Gale E. Cripe, Sr.
Orland, California

Our Double Outhouse

I grew up on a farm that had a double outhouse or privy. I never saw any like it on any farm.

Ours was a five holer, all under the same roof. The ladies' side had three holes, two large ones and a small and low one for children.

The other side for men had two holes, a wall diveded the two. Each had an outside door and each a crescent near the top. This was for ventilation. Most outhouses were north of the home due to the south wind in the summertime to keep down odor.

If the hole was dug deep enough before the privy was put over it we didn't have much fly or odor.

Lime and wood ashes were put in the holes from time to time. The ladies' side had a wooden box between the seats to hold a Sears Roebuck catalog. The mens' side had a good supply of corn cobs.

Nellie Smith
Tabor, Iowa

Brand New Outhouse

It was a wonderful day at our house in the little coal mining town of Reliance, Wyoming, when the old Union Pacific coal truck pulled out back and placed a brand new outhouse over the hole where the old one once stood. Whether paid or furnished it was a proud day for us. Ours was dark green in color but that really didn't matter. On Mondays, after mom would finish her clotheslines full of wash it was the girls' turn to take the strong, soapy lye water and either scrub the outhouse or the back porch. The seats in the outhouse or the porch would turn white after so many scrubbings, anyway.

The most exciting day for me was one day I saw mom and dad smiling and whispering, and the next thing I knew there was a small pile of wood outside the outhouse door, along with some nails and a hammer. Then dad began working on a miniature seat just for me. Twelve inches high and twelve inches wide and a six inch hole right in the middle. What a proud day for me!

Mrs. Irene (Bucho) Thiemann
Torrington, Wyoming

CHAPTER 2: What's In A Name?

The Birdhouse

At every family gathering we enjoy remembering about a family gathering at my husband's parents several years ago. We had finished our carry-in dinner. The men and children had gone outside. While the women picked up and put stuff away, our visiting was interrupted by our three-year-old granddaughter, Kelly. She came running in and grabbed great-grandma's hand, saying, "Grandma, Grandma, come quick, Uncle Doug just went into your birdhouse!"

We all looked at each other as great-grandma and Kelly went outside. Wasn't long until great-grandma came back in with a big smile on her face. The birdhouse turned out to be the outhouse! We now call the outhouse the birdhouse.

Marguerite Ryman
Kincaid, Kansas

Little House By the Stream

Our ancestry is Dutch. Dad was elated when he was told that our original family name meant "little house by the stream." He thought it so picturesque. Finally, he met someone from Holland and they told him the story about our name. The gentleman asked the original spelling, then explained (as kindly as possible) that it did indeed mean "little house by the stream," which in the Netherlands is a polite way of saying "outhouse."

Frances Bekins Dalton
New Orleans, Louisiana

Hole House

Our family loves to camp. At least twice a year we go to Brook Cherith Church Camp. The side we like to camp on is real rustic, no electricity, no plumbing, but there is an outhouse.

One day as we were preparing to go out on the lake fishing, a little girl walked by. She was holding onto her mother's hand, talking up a storm, when suddenly she paused and said, "Mommie. I have to use the HOLE HOUSE!" From that day forward the outhouse became the hole house to our family.

Jean Phelps
Dowagiac, Michigan

Closet Confusion

The little house on the back was also called the "closet" among many other names. When I was about four, my mother changed the sheets and cases on the bed, rolled up the soiled ones and told me to take them to the closet, meaning the inside clothes closet. So I did as she said.

A few hours later my mother had reason to go to the little house on the back. She naturally looked in the hole and she saw something white that shouldn't be there. You guessed it, the "sheets."

La Dean Robinson
Ceres, California

Open Door Policy

We called the outhouse the "house with the open door" as kids. After many years our small town got sewers put in. So soon we had a bathroom. My brothers took down the outhouse and covered it up. We had a Christmas wreath so we had a funeral service for the passing of the outhouse.

Thora Crowfoot
Edgewater, Colorado

Fish House Folly

Even though my nephew Mark is an eighteen-year-old young

man now, we still laugh over this incident that happened when he was about three years old.

Mark was visiting his grandparents for a few days. He had never been exposed to an outhouse, the closest thing that resembled one were the fish houses his uncles and grandfather used for ice fishing. My brother, Mark, and I went to visit some relatives who still did not have indoor plumbing.

Upon our arrival, Gertrude treated us to watermelon. It didn't take too long before Mark, very politely, asked to use the bathroom. Gertrude took Mark out the door and "down the path" to the outhouse. When they returned, Gertrude was laughing so much it took some time before she could relate what happened. When Mark got into the outhouse, he looked around and said to Gertrude, "This is a nice bathroom BUT it sure would make a good FISH HOUSE!"

Marlene Larson
Slayton, Minnesota

Visiting the Sheriff

When I was a child on our Nebraska farm, I remember Dad saying, with a little grin, that he was going to the "Sheriff's Office." I didn't know what he meant until Mother told me that it was the outhouse. Sometimes, someone would come to our front door to see Dad. Mom would send me out the back door, behind the washhouse, and back to the "Sheriff's Office" to get Dad.

I am married now and have children of my own. They have had the privilege of visiting Grandpa and Grandma on their farm. They thought it was really neat to get to use the "Sheriff's Office." My daughter was talking to Grandma a few weeks ago and wondered what Grandpa found out at the "police." Mom and I couldn't figure out what she was talking about until we remembered she was talking about the "Sheriff's Office," none other than the old OUTHOUSE.

Rosemary Holloway
Vancouver, Washington

Neighborly Neighbor

During the war my husband was frozen on the job. Every house we had lived in had been sold out from under us. We decided to buy. The only one we could get into with what money we had did not have an indoor toilet. We had a little white two holer in the back yard.

One day before going to work my husband told me to be sure and put some paper out there. So on returning from the store I had my little boy take a roll out to "Mrs. Jones," as that was what we called the outhouse.

That evening my husband hollered for paper. I couldn't understand what had happened to the paper. On questioning our little boy as to what had happened to it, to my surprise he had taken it to a neighbor (Mrs. Jones). She was out of town and her husband thought we had borrowed it.

At the next P.T.A. she laughingly told me she knew what had happened, as before she was married they called their outhouse Mrs. Jones, too.

Dora Kennedy
Colorado Springs, Colorado

Visiting Mrs. Jones

When nature called and my grandmother had to make a trip to the little house out back, she always said, "I must go see Mrs. Jones."

One day my mother and grandmother were cutting out a dress. My grandmother came across a pattern she no longer wanted. She handed the tissue pieces to my four-year-old brother and said, "Take these down to Mrs. Jones."

My brother was gone awhile and when he came back he said, "I couldn't find Mrs. Jones anywhere!"

Mrs. Emma Coulter
Springfield, Missouri

CHAPTER 3: A Place of Refuge

Pulling An "Aunt Gertrude"

My father had a spinster cousin, who helped with dishwashing until pots and pans were to be washed. She'd suddenly "need" to go to the "little house." On the way, she'd explore the chicken coop, the flower garden and whatever would delay her until the dishwashing was finished. It became a saying that anyone who left the dishwashing job was pulling an "Aunt Gertrude."

Carol Stevens
Sargent, Nebraska

Kicking The Habit

Back in the '30s my sister and I were little girls. We were old enough to do the supper dishes but we didn't like to do them. Every night after supper we would have to go out to the little house out back. We would talk, sing and stay out until Mommy would do the dishes.

One night Daddy thought he would break us of that habit. He put a white sheet over himself and stood at the corner of a building. We had to go by the building to get to the house. It scared the daylight out of us. Every night after that we did the dishes.

Mrs. Thomas Seeley
Farber, Missouri

Delaying Dishes

I was raised on a farm in Arkansas by my strict grandmother and Uncle Rob. My sister and I were about nine and twelve years old and one of our "chores" was to wash and dry the dishes right after eating and no loitering around.

I found a way to "dread it awhile." I would go down to the privy and look at the Sears Roebuck catalogue.

Then one day Uncle Rob came to the privy and propped a post up against the door so I couldn't get out. Boy, was I scared! I thought he would leave me there all day. After some crying and yelling I got out, and that cured the delay of doing dishes. To this day I do my dishes right after eating.

Rosine Hartley
Anadarko, Oklahoma

The Reading Room

I will never forget our old three holer out back. A "Papa," "Mama," and a "Kid" one. As a child and on up I was, and still am, a great one to read. My parents never objected to my reading, so that is no excuse. But after dark I'd take the kerosene lantern, hang it on the door, take along a good supply of reading material and set and read out there by the hour. Summers I'd read till the mosquitos drove me in, and winters I'd take some old coats to wrap around my legs and shoulders to help keep warm till my mother yelled it was bedtime.

Why that smelly old place was so attractive when our nice warm house was so much more comfortable, I'll never know. That old three holer still stands. If only it could talk.

Ethel Olson
Hixton, Wisconsin

True Romance

Our "little house out back," better known as the "Jones house," where we would say we were "going to visit the Joneses," had a star on the back and a little moon over the door. My oldest sister always seemed to get the calling to "visit the Joneses" right after a meal, when dishes were to be done. She still has that habit. We did find out why she stayed in there so long. She found mom's "forbidden-for-us-to-read" true romances. We got her to do a few things for us by threatening to tell on her.

Our outhouse didn't have a cement base. When the pit was full, dad would dig a new pit someplace else and move the outhouse. He used the dirt from the new pit to fill in the old one. This was the time the outhouse was repaired and painted.

I remember hearing my older "romance-reading" sister screaming at the top of her voice. Mother and all of us kids ran out, just sure she had fallen in the pit, only to find her standing on the seat. On the floor was a large bull snake. She had been so engrossed in the true romance that she didn't see the snake crawl in. When it touched her bare feet, the forbidden book was dropped. Mother killed the snake with a hoe, and needless to say we couldn't blackmail our sister with the romance magazine any more.

Cleda Baker
Caldwell, Kansas

Father's Shrine

My family grew up about a mile from the city, yet we had the convenience of indoor plumbing. Nevertheless, the old outhouse remained out back. My father must have foreseen the future, for he was blessed with his wife and four daughters. He knew what he was in for — standing in line to use the bathroom. It got increasingly worse as we became teenagers. My father would always say, "With five women in the house, the outhouse stays."

As we grew older and moved out of the house, one would have thought he would tear the eyesore down (Mother was in hope). Again, my father was thinking. All of us live in the same city and are frequent visitors to their home. He is now blessed with four granddaughters. Our city has grown up around my parents' home and they are now annexed into it. They have a lovely grassy yard, with bushes and a large garden spot. To the right of all this is a large wooden fence and there beside the fence stands the outhouse. It sits there like a shrine. Who knows, maybe he foresees great-granddaughters. I just know that the old outhouse will always be a part of the homestead.

Karen Collins
Laramie, Wyoming

Paper Dolls

As a child I was raised on a farm in Nebraska. Times were hard, but our family was proud of our outhouse because it seemed sturdier and more appealing, and maybe even warmer, than most in the neighborhood. My Dad had the WPA build it, it even had a concrete floor, one hole and was stuccoed on the ouside. With one window and two vents, it was attractive as far as outhouses go. It did not require moving to a new hole as others did, all that was necessary was to pour lime down the hole.

My sister and I spent many hours in the outhouse cutting out paper dolls from the catalogues that were used in place of tissue. It embarrassed our parents when upon an infrequent call on a neighbor we would ask them if they had an out-dated catalogue we could have. Actually we weren't asking for the catalogue for use in the outhouse as one would naturally surmise, but for more of a variety of paper dolls.

Twyla Allen
Quenemo, Kansas

Monopolized By Monopoly

My girlfriend and I love to play Monopoly. Guess where we played the game? You guessed it, in the outhouse. She sat on one hole, me on the other with the game between us. If anyone had to use it we got out until they got through, then we went back in and played some more. We laugh about that to this day, and our children think we are crazy.

Nancy Smith
Richmond, Missouri

Memories With Mom

When I was young both of our parents worked hard, but Mom was always busy with gardening, canning, feeding, cleaning, sewing, baking, mending, cooking, and all the other activities that limited finances required. At the time, I had a younger sister and an older brother, and it seemed to me that they always had more attention than I did.

But after supper when the dishes were done, Mom and I went to the outhouse together! I can see as clearly as if I were there, every crook in the path getting there and the view from the outhouse door. It was there Mom and I had some very special talks.

In the summer we would watch for lightning bugs, look at the sky and listen to the sound of trucks on the highway a mile away. Even in winter we would light the kerosene lantern and head for the outhouse. Then we talked about the stillness of winter and the beauty of snow. Occasionally we would hear a coyote in the distance, but I was never afraid when Mom was with me.

If I had any concerns or problems at school that day, that was the time I discussed them with Mom. She even shared some of her secrets with me and that made me feel very special.

Considering the way things are today, this may sound strange. But the outhouse will never fade as far as I'm concerned. It will always remind me of special memories.

Leona Shadle
Green, Kansas

Exasperated Cook

This true story has been told down through the years about my husband's parents. This happened about 45 years ago in southeast Missouri.

Every day when Dad came home from work, he immediately made his way down the path with his newspaper, to the little house out back. There he stayed for a long, long time. The family patiently, or rather impatiently, waited while their supper got colder and colder. Finally, Mom decided something must be done, so she had a plan. The next day, Dad came in from work and followed his usual habit.

Mom waited a few minutes until she was sure Dad was settled. Then she quietly slipped down through the woods and came up behind the outhouse. There was a knot hole in a board on the outhouse, directly behind where Dad sat. Mom poked a stick through the knot hole, touching Dad as she yelled out loudly, "SNAKE!" Dad sprang up, grabbed his overalls with both hands and ran for his life. What a shock! Needless to say, Dad didn't tarry in the outhouse anymore and Mom didn't have to reheat supper.

Mary Chatman
Yakima, Washington

Liver Night

My first recollection of the old outhouse was that I always had to go out there on "liver" night. It was practically a standing rule at our house that we had liver and bread and gravy for supper at least once a week. Now liver was about the least favorite food of mine that my mother could possibly make, so as soon as supper began I needed to go out there, and especially when my dad was working in the field it would be dark at suppertime and my mom had to go along with me and we would have to take a flashlight.

It took mother awhile, but she finally caught on to my little trick that it was always on liver night that I needed to go — and when she did, that was the end of my little trips out to the outhouse at suppertime.

Viola Lucht
Milford, Illinois

The Walls Have Ears

One evening my sister and I were naughty and received our punishment, but we didn't accept it like we should have, which is why we got another one. We went out to the outhouse (mad) and were telling each other how bad mother was, not knowing she was listening on the outside. Well, we got it again. This time we behaved.

I sure don't miss the outhouse except when the modern deal sitting in the bathroom gets plugged up and causes all kinds of unthinkable trouble. Then you wonder if the outhouse might still be best.

Martha Plank
Arcola, Illinois

Peeping Tom

Our home was small, without much privacy, so often when I received a letter from my fiance — off to the outhouse I'd go to read it. A time or two I felt as though I had company. There peeping through a crack in the wall was my sister reading along. I was irritated, but didn't hold a grudge long as I thought a lot of my sister.

The Montgomery Ward or Sears catalogue served as our toilet paper. I don't think the black newsprint rubbed off on you as today's does.

Ruth McMillan
Buffalo, Missouri

Spit And Shine

When I was nine years old it was the worst year of the Depression for our family of eight. We moved to the country from the city. My Daddy could work for Mr. S. for sixty cents a day and a house to live in. Mr. and Mrs. S. had no children. They took a liking to me. Mrs. S. wanted me to stay days and help with small chores. They both took long naps and rested every day after lunch and I had nothing to do. At first I wandered outside missing my two sisters and little brothers. Nature called. I went to the outhouse, and as I sat on the seat I saw right across from me a little knot hole about the size of a dime in the wall.

I spit at the hole. Of course I missed. I spit again and I missed again. Well, it takes a while to make spit, but I kept trying to spit in that hole. Every day as soon as Mr. and Mrs. S. went to bed I would see how many times out of ten I could hit that hole. I thought Mrs. S. wouldn't mind me spitting on the wall, since every day or so she would have me take the broom and a bucket of warm soapy water and wash the seat and floor of the outhouse, then open the seat lid and put in a little lime. She wanted the outhouse fresh and clean. I thought I better wash the wall since I spit on it. Then I decided she might wonder why I only washed one wall. I washed all the walls as far as I could reach.

One day I overheard Mrs. S. telling my Mother what a good worker I was, saying, "She not only washes the seat and floor, she washes the walls!"

Mrs. Glen Hancock
Bois D'Arc, Missouri

Congenial Meeting Place

I recall how us cousins would love to all go to the outhouse at the same time when we visited at Uncle Bert's farm. He was a great hand at doing things different, and built a large outhouse. In the center he had this square about 4 feet by 4 feet, and on each corner was a hole. Four of us could sit at once, and sit we did and talk, tell stories, and have many good laughs. Seemed like a congenial meeting place — never knew another one like it. It was unique!

Mrs. Leo Strouth
Brewster, Minnesota

Heard It Through the Grapevine

Outhouses! What pungent memories the topic arouses. Not only because of their obvious purpose, but also from the conferences that took place there.

I was the sentinel just outside the door of ours during my sixth through ninth years after the huge family dinners. My mother and aunts would go two by two through the garden gate, along a path having the grape arbor on one side and beds of dill and sage on the other, until they reached the sanctuary of the outhouse in the lower corner. They took me along so I could let them know if anyone was approaching as they gossiped about all the other

30

relatives; what they wore, what dishes they had brought to the dinner, how they looked and how their children behaved. This went on until every possible combination of women had discussed the others. Sometimes two would stay too long and two others would have to stop along the path to make their observations. Seeing me posted at the door would alert them to keep out of hearing distance.

If these conferences could have been taped and played back, they surely would have put an end to the infamous institution of family dinner.

Jo Buddenberg
Hamilton, Missouri

Cheating Doesn't Pay

When we were first married, nearly 42 years ago, we had one of those old outhouses. One evening, friends came to play cards. As usual the men played against the women and they were beating us. My friend and I went to the outhouse. While we were there we made up signals so we could beat the men. But no, we couldn't beat them. We later found that they stood outside and listened to what we were going to do. It certainly doesn't pay to cheat.

Name Withheld
Goodland, Kansas

Brothers Made Beautiful Music

So, we're on the subject of outhouses, way, way back. I had three brothers and the old outhouse had room for three. After supper when it was dark, they would all go to the outhouse to "sit." They took their harmonicas along and sat down. Then we heard the greatest concerts as all three of them played song after song on their mouth harps. I wish I had tapes of those concerts. They were beautiful.

Mrs. Tena Foth
Hillsboro, Kansas

Our Own Security System

We lived on a farm in Kansas about twelve miles from town. My sister was ten years old and I was seven. In the winter time our folks would leave early in the morning while the ground was still frozen with the wagon and horses. They did the shopping and had to wait until the ground was frozen over again before they started to come back home, so by then it was getting dark. My sister and I were afraid to stay in the large house after dark so we would light a lantern and go out to the "little house in the back," and stay and look at the Sears and Montgomery Ward catalogues to pass the time. I guess we thought we were safer in there rather than in the house!

Virginia Anderson
El Cajon, California

Outhouse Provided Much-Needed Sanctuary

A number of years ago the Santa Fe Railroad had a small passenger train that stopped in our small community in Oklahoma. We affectionately called it the "doodlebug."

We had an elderly neighbor who lived with his daughter who needed to make a trip to Kansas City to be with her daughter during childbirth. She didn't want to leave her dad alone, so despite his protests she had arranged for him to ride the "doodlebug" to Shawnee to stay with relatives.

As the hour drew near for the doodlebug to make its local stop, the old gentleman became more adamant about not making the trip. The daughter was determined he should go, but while she was busy, this clever old fellow slipped out to the outhouse and locked himself in. All her pleading and tears were to no avail.

The doodlebug came and went, but it was minus one elderly passenger who used the outhouse as a much-needed sanctuary.

Peggy Whitt
Burbank, Oklahoma

The Dating Game

This happened to a very dear friend when we were both

young girls. The boys at this time would go to the girl's home and ask for a date, always on Sunday evening. One Sunday evening this friend had nothing better to do so she went to the outhouse and she was taking her time reading the catalogue. In the meantime a car with two young men drove in the yard. One of the men wanted to date this young girl. He went to the house and asked for her. The mother said, "Well, she is around here somewhere. She will be here soon."

The young lady saw the car and the young man, and she decided just to stay in the outhouse until they left. But to her surprise, they didn't leave. So finally she had to come out and greet the boys. She was so embarrassed, she knew she didn't smell like a rose after being in the outhouse.

The young man asked her for a date and she said yes, if he would give her time to clean up. A year later they were married and spent many happy years together.

Pauline Becker
Russell, Kansas

Embarassing Explanation

The family car disappeared down the lane on the way to the big Fourth of July celebration at the county seat, leaving the two daughters of the family waiting for their young men to call for them.

The girls decided to make a final trip "down the path." No more had they reached their destination than their swains roared in.

"If we had just come right on out," they wailed later. "But we were embarassed. And the longer we waited, the more impossible it was!"

So, peeking through a crack in the door, they watched as their escorts went to the house repeatedly to knock on the door, then returned to the car to wait.

Minutes dragged on. The heat was stifling. Finally, after a last trip to the door, the Model T drove off in a cloud of dust, and the wilted, tearful girls crept out.

Not only did they miss the long anticipated Fourth of July celebration, but they had to think up a plausible explanation. Of course they had a long quiet day in which to do this.

The truth has never been told till now —

Ruth Boellstorff
Brock, Nebraska

Surprise Package

My most embarrassing moment was after I was grown and had gone to the city to work.

One weekend I came home on an early morning bus which stopped at a service station on the highway to let me off. My Dad didn't know I was coming on that bus and the station operator hadn't come to open up the building. There was no place for me to wait out of the cold. I noticed the outhouse, left my bag at the station door and went to the outhouse to wait. In a short while I heard footsteps, the door opened and there I set. He (the station operator) had noticed my baggage and decided to investigate. After explanations and a good laugh, I called home and was soon picked up by my Dad. Needless to say, I will never forget the little house out back.

Eudema Smith
Shawnee, Kansas

Sinful Steps

The old outbuilding was a fact of life sixty years ago in southern Missouri, where I grew up.

At the country school I attended we had a big five holer built to straddle a draw. The holes ranged from great big to a tiny first grader one. Made of unpainted oak, the faded grey color of the outhouse blended pleasantly with the green of the trees sheltering it.

About the time I was in the fifth grade the Charleston filtered down to our backwoods community. The dance was frowned upon by the adults as sinful.

After several of the girls had picked up a step or two, we'd race to the outbuilding at recess time to practice. One at a time we stood in front of the rest of the girls, seated solemnly between the holes, and strut our stuff. All of us agreed that the little blond first grader who only knew one step was by far the best. The rest of us lacked rhythm. We had no music, and we never thought of clapping to create a rhythm.

The one-by-twelve oak boards stretched across the ravine resounded mightily to our stomping and twisting. One day the teacher heard it. She came down the hill to see what in the world the girls were doing all this time. Caught in the act, we all performed as best we could in spite of our embarassment. Sinning was serious business in our neighborhood.

After our promise never to do the Charleston again, she walked back to the schoolhouse grinning from ear to ear. We were true to our promise to the teacher.

Mary Hamilton Neary
Wichita, Kansas

CHAPTER 4: Pesky Critters

All Your Ducks In A Row

We spent part of our honeymoon with some friends in the wilds of Wisconsin. They had a big, old farm home with an outhouse — not out in back, but in front and a little south of the driveway. The outhouse, itself, was a shock to the city girl I was then, as I had never used one. The embarrassment of having to cross the driveway and go past the machine shed where someone was usually working was bad enough. Total humiliation came when a large, waddling duck, quacking loudly to her three chicks bobbing along in a row behind her, followed me to the outhouse every time I got up the courage to make the trip. I felt as though I was leading a noisy parade! The worst time was yet to come! One morning the ducks and I made our procession to the outhouse in the usual manner. While I was in the outhouse I heard a truck drive up and park about 30 feet away from it. I just couldn't make myself walk out of that place while several strange men were standing there talking to our friend. I waited, hoped, and prayed that they would go away. Finally, they all went into the machine shed. I peeked out and saw that they were busy way back in the shed so thought I could sneak out quietly with no one noticing me. I opened the door quietly and started to run for the house when that darn duck and her little ones set up the most awful clatter. I could hear the men laughing all the way to the house, and when I got in the house my new husband and the women were roaring with laughter. I thought for a second what a silly sight the ducks and I had made, scuttling into the house, and began to giggle myself. Believe me, it was a joke our friends never let me forget.

Catherine Chapman
Harshaw, Wisconsin

Fowl Play

The old outhouse is quite vivid in my memory, especially the cold winters, or during an electrical storm. One outstanding incident that is told often in our family doesn't pertain to either of these, however.

We lived on a farm in northeastern Kansas. I had three older sisters, so when I needed to go out back there was always someone to go with me, because we had an old hen that would attack me. Even after her chicks were grown she would flogg and peck me.

One fall after my sisters started to school, I asked my mother to accompany me, but she was busy canning and couldn't leave it. She told me to pick up a stick and hit her if she started after me.

I went out the door very quietly, but there was no stick in sight. When I was about halfway to my destination, I heard it coming. I was by the woodpile so I picked up a stick of cookstove wood and swung for her head. She staggered a ways then dropped. I was afraid, for it wasn't the hen but the big Rhode Island rooster. I didn't see how I could hide anything that big. I then remembered where I had started to go. I drug him in and managed to drop him in a hole. I didn't say a word to mother about it.

It wasn't long until father came home for lunch. As soon as he got in the door he asked what was wrong with the rooster, that he was making an awful fuss about something. They decided they had best go check. I decided right quick that I had best tell them what I knew. It turned out what I thought was a dead rooster was only stunned, and when he came to he was a very unhappy rooster. Father opened the service door on the back of the outhouse and set it free.

My parents didn't waste any time about substituting the stick of stovewood with a lighter weight stick. They didn't want me to knock out anymore of their chickens.

Vera Howard
Grants, New Mexico

Unwelcome Guests

My father was a farmer in Iowa. The banker had several farms, so we lived on one of them. Our outhouse was built at one end of the chickenhouse. First time some of us went to the outhouse, we felt what we thought was splinters. It happened every time, so one day mom decided to smooth the boards of the seat. That's when she found that our splinters were really chicken lice that came from the chickenhouse! So daddy had to build another one several feet from the old one. We were so happy about not getting bitten.

Alice Mayfield
Mesa, Arizona

Tom Turkey

It was about 1936 and times were pretty tough. Mother raised a few turkeys to be dressed and sold to get us a little money for Christmas.

Of course we had a large "Prize Turkey Gobbler." He had a wide wingspread and enjoyed chasing me with wings spread as I carried a bucket of eggs.

He delighted in catching someone in the "outhouse" and wouldn't let them out. When you yelled for help he just gobbled all the louder and no one could hear you.

One day company came from several miles away. So of course the ladies headed for the little path. Shortly we heard "Old Tom" gobble, gobble, gobble out there, so all rushed out to shoo him away and rescue the ladies. Mother was so embarrassed.

Mrs. Gene Turner
Ponca City, Oklahoma

Riding The Storm Out

During the war in 1944 we bought our first house out in the country. All we had was a shell of a house and an outhouse.

A friend gave us a hen with twelve baby chickens, and the only place we had to keep them was in the outhouse.

One night a violent thunderstorm came up, the lightning and thunder was terrific and the wind blew a gale. I was looking out the window and saw the outhouse turn over.

I spoke to my husband tearfully, "The outhouse just blew over, all my baby chickens will drown."

We rushed out in our night clothes, and after lifting the heavy building, we found mama and babies still in their box just a little damp. They spent the rest of the night in the house with us.

E.R. Raber
Benton, Arkansas

Lost Love

I was five years old and cornered in our little outhouse by the neighbor's red rooster. Everytime I opened the door to go out, he flew at me. I screamed and cried until finally the rooster's owner rescued me. He walked me to our door with that horrible creature tucked under his arm, and told my mom, "He wants to fight anything today. I killed one of his favorite hens this morning for chicken and dumplings."

Norma Moore
Belleville, Illinois

Stampeding Sows

My earliest memories, when I was really quite young, are of an old farmhouse in Iowa. It is the first house I remember living in. It had a big yard and lots of trees, and a little old shack out back.

Lots of memories include cousins, and one incident includes a particular cousin a few years younger than myself.

It was a warm summer day, very warm, maybe a holiday like the Fourth of July.

My city cousin was visiting with her parents. We had done all the things people do when company comes. In the natural course of events in the middle of that long hot afternoon, after several glasses of Kool-aid, my cousin and I reluctantly decided to stroll down the ol' boardwalk to the little ol' shack out back — also known as the outhouse.

Now, neither of us was too enthusiastic about taking that walk, especially not my city cousin who was used to a little more modern way. However, when you have to, you have to.

Well, we got there and went in. We immediately decided not to stay any longer than necessary because it was even warmer in there than outside.

Besides, there were spiders in there, which neither one of us were too crazy about, and well, the smell wasn't anything to write home about. Anyway, my cousin was scared, and since I was the oldest, I had to be brave.

We were just about to leave when there was a terrible thundering noise and the ground started shaking. Suddenly, a raging stampede of sows came around the corner. I stopped being brave right then.

Without discussion, a unanimous decision was made to stay and suffer the heat, smell and spiders rather than face those monster pigs. The decision to scream and cry was almost as instantaneous as the one to shut the door.

It seemed like hours before our parents came to our rescue, although I suppose it wasn't very long. It must have been a very traumatic experience, though, since my cousin still remembers and she's younger than I am and I was very young at the time.

Vickie Beyer
Barnes City, Iowa

Mondays In The Throne Room

When our sons were young boys they belonged to a 4-H club and had a few sheep. We lived on a farm and I had to use a clothesline prop with a rope clothesline. For some unknown reason the ram didn't like this pole, and just as soon as I put this prop in place to keep my clothes in the breeze and off the ground he would charge after me. I did not have time to get to the house, so would go for the outhouse. He would keep guard over me. From the cracks in the siding of the outhouse I also kept a nervous watch over him, all the while hoping he'd not hit the place. He never did. I couldn't get out, so there I'd sit the rest of the day until the boys came home from school and they heard me calling them, also saw the ram circling the outhouse or standing at the door. Needless to say after a couple of Mondays in the throne room, my husband put a fence around the yard to keep the ram confined to his quarters. Whenever my sons want to tell a funny story about mom they always tell about how mom likes her outhouse.

Loretta Morgan
Phillipsburg, Kansas

An Uplifting Experience

One evening after school when I was about to mount my horse to go home I noticed the owner of the barn, Mr. Stout, a man probably in his late sixties, was entering the outhouse that was a short distance from the barn. He had just about enough time to get well seated on the big hole when Joe, my horse, started backing like a runaway horse toward the gentleman in the outhouse, and before I knew what was happening there was a loud blast that sounded like crashing thunder after a big flash of lightning, and I could see the outhouse being raised up off the foundation with the old gentleman in it.

By the time I was in control we were already down the road heading for home. To tell you the truth I didn't know what to do — laugh or cry. I was so embarrassed that I didn't tell anyone for a long time, but the word did get around as there had been a witness. To this day I have wondered what Mr. Stout's reactions were and what he thought had happened.

Could it have been an earthquake in Wilmore, Kansas?

Marie Swisher
Coldwater, Kansas

No Appreciation

It was always a joke with my two brothers and sister that anytime I was in there (the outhouse) I would sing real loud, not caring who heard me. So the real joke is that one of the cows (Reddy, we called her) didn't seem to like me and I suppose my singing either, and she would stand at the outhouse door, paw the ground and make noises to let you know she was mad and disgusted.

So later I was ready to get out. I'd start yelling for help, so the boys could chase her away. But those two guys would let me stay for awhile or until mother made them come to my rescue.

Elsie Reiter
Phoenix, Arizona

Hickory Dickory Dock

In the late 1930's we lived on a farm with an "outhouse." I was a young girl at that time but I will never forget one day when I went to "visit" the outhouse and had put a coat on as it was cold. While sitting there a mouse ran down the sleeve of my coat. I have never moved that fast before or after that day! The thing I don't remember is if I ever finished what I went out there for in the first place!

Marlene Fey
Papillion, Nebraska

Double Impressions

Here is my early memory of the outhouse.

The day I wasn't alone! Back in the 1930's a trip to the outhouse in seasonable weather served a dual purpose. There I would slip into a dream world of my own, thoroughly enjoying flipping through the pages of the Sears Roebuck and Montgomery Ward catalogs, viewing the fashionable shoes. Yes, someday when I grew up among my possessions would be a pair of shiny shoes of every obtainable color. As I sat covering the round hole in the board seat, a glimpse of reality flickered back as my eyes dropped to the corner of the floor, and a moment of panic and fear struck.

There lay a curled up huge snake! I screamed and ran out the door with the round impression on my backside and memories of that moment of fear. The sound of shrieking laughter in the distance came from my younger brother. If I could have caught him he might have had a few bruises and felt lucky not to be like the snake — dead.

Viola Gallentine
Norton, Kansas

Rattled By A Rattlesnake

When I was a young girl growing up in Texas, we had an outhouse. One day I made my way to the outhouse. I thought someone might be in there ahead of me, so I cautiously peeked in a hole in the door. To my surprise, on the area next to the seat, there was a good sized rattlesnake coiled. I ran back to the house, and shouted for my brother to come and shoot that snake. We all laugh about the incident now, but at that time it was not so funny. I am just glad I wasn't in a hurry that day.

Mrs. Steven Lange
Rowena, Texas

Little "Darlings"

One Sunday my husband's family gathered at his folks' for one of there "get togethers." After a wonderful meal the children all went outside and the women went busily about their usual routine of putting away all the food and doing the dishes.

His folks had one of the famous "WPA" little houses out back. They also had the cutest little white Angora kittens. Soon we heard a loud commotion outside. We all went immediately to see what the trouble was. You could never guess. ALL OUR LITTLE DARLINGS had thrown those white kittens down the deep holes in the "little house out back."

Grandpa was furious! He sent the kids to the house to get some pieces of meat while he got a small pail and placed a rope on the handle. He would put a piece of meat in the pail and lower it down the hole. When the kitten jumped into the pail for the meat

43

he would pull each one up.

This accomplished, he lined the kids all up together and I'm sure they will never forget the lecture they got from Grandpa.

Mrs. R.A. Cundall
Murray, Nebraska

Myrtle The Turtle

The boys' outhouse provided an unexpected lesson in sex education. One recess, the boys came rushing to the schoolhouse to report that a turtle had fallen into the outhouse pit. To lift the hapless turtle from its predicament, we used a hoe which I kept for killing the unwelcome rattlesnakes that sometimes invaded our playground. A bath at the windmill soon made the turtle presentable again, and the students clamored to keep it. They provided water, lettuce, bits of bread, and a few grasshoppers; and the turtle thrived. Of course, a pet turtle must have a name. Taking an idea from a popular cartoon, someone suggested "Myrtle, the Turtle." "Oh, no!" piped up a kindergarten boy. "We can't name him that. He was in the boys' toilet." The rest of the students acceded and selected the name Tommy. Tommy lived happily at school until the end of the year when he was released at a nearby pond.

Mae Rose King
Lewellen, Nebraska

Cats On Parade

The other outhouse that I remember fondly, is the one on a small farm where we lived for a short time. We had two mother cats with assorted kittens, and they always would follow anyone whenever we walked out to the outhouse, walking in a row behind us like a parade. If we stayed in it too long, the kittens would poke their little furry paws under the door, to remind us that they were waiting for us. We were used to this performance, but it startled some of our visitors when those little paws came reaching under the door while they were inside. It was a good way to know whether or not the "little house" was occupied, as we had only to look for the row of cats and kittens waiting outside its door to know that someone was using it.

U.R. LeRoy
Corunna, Michigan

Maternal Mother

I had an experience in the outhouse I'll never forget.

A few years back when we still lived on the farm I was working in my garden one evening. I needed to go to the bathroom, and to save time rather than walk to the house I went to the old outhouse, which was closer.

I didn't know that one of our many farm cats had made a maternity ward under the floor boards of the outhouse. When she heard me unroll the toilet paper it scared her and she came clawing up out of the hole I was sitting on. I got up real fast, but not before I had several good scratch marks. From then on I never used the outhouse again.

Mrs. O. Willour
Ransom, Kansas

Smelled Like Roses By Supper

My memory of the outhouse is when my daughter, ten, was sitting out there with her dog and she was always sicking the dog on everything. There came a bumble bee in so she sicked the dog on it and it went in the next hole so the dog went right in after it. When the dog finally got out, she went shaking all the way to the house. I guess you know we had a clean-up job to do on her, sidewalks and also the dog.

She is 46 now and we still get a big laugh over that. At the time I could of run off instead of cleaning them up.

It wasn't funny at all at the time as I was having company for supper.

As I remember now, everyone was smelling like a rose by supper time.

Marcena Leathers
Delta, Iowa

Left The Light "On"

One night I had extra kitchen work to do. My husband and children had been in bed for some time when I had to go to the outhouse. So I lit the lantern and away I went. The door on the outhouse opened in instead of out. I pushed it open put the lantern down, turned around and the door moved, and here came a skunk. I had closed it in when I opened the door. I took out on high, leaving the lantern till morning. I was lucky, I could of smelled like a skunk or it could of turned the lantern over, causing a fire. This happened before we had electric power. I thought Dad and the children would never forget my experience.

Edna Hines
Rich Hill, Missouri

CHAPTER 5: Mishaps, Blunders
and Natural Disasters

Funeral Fiasco

Back in 1929 my daughter was two years old. My grandfather had died and it was the day of his funeral. We were ready to leave for the funeral, and I sent my young daughter to the outhouse. Grandpa had built it and made seats for three people. My grandpa was a very large man so one hole was very big, one smaller, then one down low for children. My daughter got up on the larger one and fell in. After a few minutes I went to see what the matter was and I had to get help to get her out and she sure was a mess to clean up before we could go on to the funeral. She has forgotten, but I never will.

F. Churches
Golden, Colorado

Safety Matches?

When my husband's sister and he were youngsters, his sister burned down their outhouse. She was probably seven or eight years old at the time. Well, she said she used safety matches and there was <u>no</u> reason for that outhouse to have burned down! That experience has been handed down for years and years.

Mrs. Harold Thompson
Gordon, Nebraska

Teeter Totter Tot

When you asked for outhouse stories I immediately thought of my niece. In our outhouse we had two holes, one adult size, one child size. When two children went, one got the larger hole. I had the smaller hole and she was teetering on the edge of the big one when all at once down she went. Her shoulders caught and there she was with her knees pressed tightly to her chin and her feet straight up. She was screaming and crying. I tried with all my strength to pull her up, but I couldn't. I ran to get her mother and after much struggling we pulled her up. Only her shoulders had saved her from a fate worse than death.

Marie Holzwarth
St. Francis, Kansas

Head Over Heels

My playmate and I decided one day, we would like to see what each other looked like, looking through the holes of the little house out back. We stood on tiptoe and each put our head through a hole. We were having fun till we decided to take our heads out. Unfortunately, the hole I had my head in had a nail underneath, headed straight for the hole, and every time I tried to get out it cut me. My playmate went running and screaming to her mother that I had my head stuck in the outhouse hole. Her mother looked the situation over and lifted me straight up by the heels.

The ordeal was over. By the way, we never decided to do that trick again.

Mrs. Luther Pomraning
Airville, Pennsylvania

Go Fish

It was the rule to keep the door open when not in use, partly to keep it aired and partly so others would know it was not in use.

Often hens would go in there, go down into the opening and make a nest on the ledge that extended all around, with the cavity in the center then fly away through the open door. Only Dad

48

could reach far enough to retrieve the eggs.

My five year-old cousin wandered into the outhouse and, ignoring the small seat, he decided to try the big two-holer. Looking down he noticed the eggs and decided to bring them to Grandma, climbed up on the big seat and leaning over lost his balance and fell into the pit underneath. Luckily, it had been cleaned recently, but still had been used several times since.

His screams brought the household running and when his mother saw he was not hurt she said, "Throw him back. He's not worth cleaning!"

Ruth Christopher
Tulsa, Oklahoma

Book Fumble

One doesn't see one of these outhouses in regular use much any more. Of course, the little town in North Dakota where I grew up in and near knew no other. Cold and drafty in the winter (snow drifted through the cracks), hot and stuffy in the summer.

In the early years of our marriage, I kept ours as clean as possible by taking the warm, sudsy water on wash day, added some Clorox and scrubbed the inside good with an old broom, especially the seat and floor. Then with a little Clorox in the rinse water, I splashed that over the sudsy areas. I remember how nice it was when my husband earned enough money to buy a roll of tissue once in a while! The little papers that the fresh crated fruit came wrapped in were a luxury, too. It wasn't until I was 32 and carrying our sixth child that we got an "indoor."

There is one story about an "outhouse" that my children thought quite funny, and now my grandchildren are as anxious for me to tell it as my children were.

Back during the depression, when I was seven, my father lost the family farm and had to move his large family into this little town. The tiny three-room house we lived in was located about a block or so from the schoolhouse. On the school grounds there was the nice horse barn for those who rode or drove to school from the country and at each end of the barn were the big His and

Hers outhouses.

I remember well the fall I was ten, when we got (what I thought was government issue) two big new "outhouses" for the school. The high seat was difficult to reach and there was a nice square, paneless window high on one side, over the seat. I was child number three in our family of seven children, and my sister and brother and I spent a lot of time together.

We were supposed to go right home after school, but once in a while we played around on the swings or merry-go-round before going home. This particular cool, crisp afternoon we stayed to play, and when "duty" called, we decided it was more fun to use the new building at the schoolhouse than to run the short distance home to our old one. Then, the first thing we knew we were throwing my Reader back and forth through the little window. We were having a good time when I, on the inside, missed. Yes — it went down the hole open side down. That was the end of the game, the fun was over. Now we had to go home and tell Mama. My, was she ever upset with me, we not only didn't come home when we should have, but we lost a costly school book. Now, Mama always knew just what to do, she put on her coat, buttoning it as we went out the door, telling me to get the garden rake and we would go get the book.

It was dark when we left that nice new "outhouse" with the book. Supper would have to wait that night. She set up the ironing board near the washstand, spread newspapers over the ironing board, took a pan of warm, soapy water and clean rags and proceeded to clean, by the light of the kerosene lamp, one page at a time. I had to stand there and watch and every little while Mama would say "Peee-uuu Fern, Pee-uu." (Since I've grown I've wondered why she didn't make me do it.)

After supper, she took warm flat irons heated on the wood range, and ironed every page in that book as I watched.

The next morning she sent me to school early, telling me to take the book, now a littler fatter, and exchange it for a different one, putting it in the back of the bookcase. We called them cupboards, they reached to the ceiling and had wainscoting doors.

All the rest of that school year, I just knew the teacher, a stern, unmarried woman, would find that book and know that I was the one responsible for its condition.

Needless to say, we three kids never lingered after school the rest of that year.

Fern Nieland
Wapato, Washington

Shiny Red Shoes

When I was ready for the third grade in 1948, we moved to a more metropolitan area. I had always gone to a country school so I knew nothing about cliques or being a new kid in strange surroundings. But I soon found the meaning of those things could make me and a couple of other new kids really feel like outsiders. One particular little girl seemed to be head princess of the elite group. She was always dressed just so and was good at letting everyone know she was super special. One day she wore red patent shoes to school. Gosh, were they ever pretty! We all had one pair of school shoes, usually black or brown so polish could cover the scuffs and make for longer wear. But here was this kid wearing red shoes to match her very pretty dress. And did she ever enjoy calling attention to that fact. When a bunch of us were at the outhouse — I think it was a three seater, very modest, the little girl went into her act again. She thought some of us had not drooled enough so she began to dance and kick her feet. You could have heard a pin drop as we watched one shiny red shoe sail through the air — drop through one hole and land kerplunk many feet below! She cried and cried because the shiny red shoe was lost forever. We had the good manners and consideration not to laugh — at least not aloud. But gosh was it funny. Unfortunately, her attitude toward other people did not undergo a miraculous change, but a lot of us had much more respect for that old outhouse from then on.

Betty Williams
Bennington, Oklahoma

Shivaree Shenanigans

In the fall of 1932, my date and I, and another couple, went to an old-fashioned charivari (shivaree) of our friends who had just been married.

After a lengthy time of yelling, beating old tubs and pans with sticks — making the usual noises made at charivaris, my girlfriend and I went to the outhouse to flip some gravel out of my shoes — flip they did! One shoe flipped down the toilet seat hole!

My girlfriend went to get our boyfriends and they retrieved the shoe, took it to the pond and washed it thoroughly!

I accepted the wet, still "highly perfumed" shoe with a red face and total embarrassment!

Now, after fifty-plus years later whenever I see my old boyfriend and his lovely wife, he winks at me, then glances down to my feet!

> Mary Tate
> Springfield, Missouri

Firmly Grounded

I was in second grade and going to a one-room country school with an outhouse in the back. My parents didn't have much money. To save wear on our shoes, we had to go to school barefooted long as the weather permitted.

On a cold, November day a little classmate and I were playing in the outhouse. I kicked my leg high as I could, my shoe came off and fell down the johnny hole. The weather was so cold, and I had to walk two miles home barefooted.

Mom sent an older brother back to school and he rescued my shoe with a fishin' pole. Mom then had to do a clean up job.

My parents didn't have to remind me after that to keep both feet on the floor in an outhouse.

> Daisy Lane
> Fair Play, Missouri

Putting On Airs

I remember our outhouse as one that was badly in need of

repair. The back side (which faced the woods to the north) had two boards missing. It did get cool in there some days.

My mother's sister and family were coming to visit from California. They had inside bathrooms so mom was after dad to fix up our outhouse before company arrived. Dad was slow. He didn't see the need to "put on airs" for our California kinfolk.

Well about a week before company arrived, most everyone had gone to the barn to do the milking (Dad was slow about that too, and usually visited the old outhouse and smoked his pipe). We all saw the smoke and ran toward the house to see if it was on fire. But no, it was the old outhouse. Mom got accused of burning it down so we could have a new one before company arrived, but we all knew Dad's habit of dusting his pipe into the hole. There was enough paper in the hole to start a fire. By the time the ashes from Dad's pipe became a blaze, he had been at the barn for some time.

We all said that was the warmest our old outhouse had ever been.

Vera Beach
Gladstone, Missouri

Guard Duty

My little cousin had the habit of throwing her panties down the hole when finished and my aunt always yelled at her and fished them out with a stick.

As we children were always scared after dark of the boogey man, we always went to the outhouse by two's walking back to back, then one stood guard duty outside.

Shirley Goodwin
Lucas, Iowa

Shangri-La

Years ago my sister and her husband bought their little two acre "estate" with a small modern farmhouse, a little red barn, a chickenhouse and an outhouse. The previous owner built the outhouse for his hired men. The little two seater was out back and off to the right of the house with its door facing the wheat fields. My sister hated it but my brother-in-law loved it. It was his Shangri-la, his library of Zane Grey books, catalogues, etc. My sister decided to make the best of it. She painted it, attached a rose trellis to the back, planted box wood, iris and tulips around the back and sides. A little pear tree already stood close to one corner. Nobody dared again to ask if she had indoor plumbing. I stopped there on my vacation. My sister was glad to see me. She was ready to can pears. The jars were sterilized, and the little pear tree's branches were bending down with big beautiful ripe pears. Since it was a weekend we decided to relax and visit. Sunday afternoon we were sitting on the porch when we smelled smoke and heard my brother-in-law yelling for the hose. My sister grabbed the hose and ran around the house. There he stood holding his pants up with one hand, a Zane Grey in the other. The outhouse was on fire. The hose wouldn't reach. My sister was laughing so hard she was rolling on the grass. In time we got our wits together, attached another hose and put out the fire. There were no more pears. Later my brother-in-law admitted that while he was sitting there reading and throwing cigarette butts down the toilet he had forgotten that several days earlier he emptied a pan of motor oil in the outhouse.

O.M. Roth
Silver Spring, Maryland

Gypsy Guests

Gypsies had gone by that day and finding no one home made use of the outhouse, dropping their cigarettes in the day old catalog paper. We had inside plumbing so we didn't need it any more. It was a good thing as a large hole was burned in the back and never seemed to be private anymore, so it was torn down.

Was my face red when fellow students would ask, "What burned?"

Irma Adams Smith
Vancouver, Washington

Firefly

The outhouse was fabulous. It was a beautiful two seater made from cedar (even the shingles on the top) from our place. The lumber had been planed (by hand) and was varnished until it glowed. The Sears catalogue had its own shelf above the large metal can that was used to hold off-casts.

One Friday afternoon my sister brought a girlfriend home with her from college. They did not want my parents to know the girlfriend smoked, so she did it in the outhouse.

On Sunday morning just before we were ready to leave for Sunday School and church, she started to the outhouse to have her last smoke before afternoon. When she started down the back porch steps she began screaming. The entire outhouse was a mass of flames and was about to fall in. So the outhouse went up in smoke.

The visitor had dropped a used, but still burning cigarette in the bin with the paper.

No, my parents were not angry, but the next outhouse was not so fancy as there was no more cedar left to make it with.

For the next forty-six years (as long as she lived), she was a friend and often came to visit. She gave herself the name "Fire Fly."

Daisy McCorkle
Vaiden, Mississippi

Outhouse Indigestion

This is an incident that may sound fictitious, but actually happened.

Our close neighbor's wife had been doing some dry cleaning with something similar to gasoline. When she had finished she poured the excess cleaning solution down one of the holes in the outhouse. Later, when her husband John went out, he lit up his pipe and threw his lighted match down the other hole. A terrible explosion followed, blowing the outhouse all to pieces and John landed out in the middle of the yard, with his clothing in embarrassing disarray. His wife, fearing the worst, called for my father for help, saying "Come quick, Floyd, come quick!"

When my father arrived very shortly, he helped John up on his feet and asked "What in the world happened to you John?" And John replied, "I don't know Floyd, it must have been something I ate."

Guy Davis
Indianola, Iowa

Had A Guardian Angel

I'm not sure if I was eight or nine years old, at the time, before my parents had a bathroom. My habit was to run to the outhouse before I went to school. One morning as I was going out there I saw a big rat at the wood pile near the outhouse. Knowing that mom's chicks were disappearing I ran back to tell my dad of the rat. He, thinking I stayed in the house, went and got the gun. I and the dog returned to the outhouse. Well, dad shot the rat. I tho't, "My that sounded close," so I looked at my arm to see if it was bleeding. All seemed well until I got up. The bullet fell from my lap. It had glanced off, and went thru the side of the outhouse into my lap, but didn't hurt anything. So child like I was, picked up the bullet in my hand, went in the house and told mom that dad shot me. Well dad and mom turned white and nearly fainted as I skipped happily to school. Years later I realized it could have been death.

I was lucky. Guess an Angel watched over me.

Name Withheld
Sarasota, Florida

Shot In The Dark

Before the days of indoor plumbing it was considered very dangerous to travel to the "North Forty" as we sometimes called it.

At this particular time our youngest son was learning to use his dad's rifle.

As he lifted the gun, as accidents usually happen, the gun went off, shelling shot thru the outhouse.

At the time dad was occupying it. He ran out very excited, and so were the rest.

Nellie Dale
Mountain View, Missouri

Between A Rock And A Hard Place

It happened when Grandpa was in the outhouse and the lower boards were off the bottom on the backside for air, and a few large stones were lying around in the back.

My mother asked my father to kill a chicken for dinner. He took his rifle and when the chicken was in his sights he pulled the trigger. The shot missed the chicken, but hit the rock in the back of the outhouse, ricocheted into the outhouse and hit Grandpa.

He came out screaming with his britches down and we all thought a wasp had stung him till we saw the blood.

He never quite forgave my father, and he never did think it was funny.

Mrs. C.G. McCallister
Baxter Springs, Kansas

The Rock of Gibraltar

On hot summer nights, the outhouse was converted into a bathhouse. This was more convenient, as it kept the mess out of our house, and was closer to the well and the big black kettle where our water was heated with a fire under it.

One particular Saturday evening, when I was five and my sister almost three, it was our important job to put the papers on the outhouse floor to set the tub on. Whenever we put them down, the wind would blow the papers up. So I had the bright idea of putting rocks down to keep the papers from blowing. My sister found a large rock and set it down, right on my big toe. How could such a little girl lift such a big rock? I can still remember the pain and later, the loss of my toenail.

Elaine Hageman
Axtell, Kansas

Early-Day Garbage Disposal

As a child we wallpapered the outhouse with scraps and pieces left from the trimmings mother had when our home walls got a face lift.

Once in a while the outhouse was a place to hide mistakes, like when forgetting the leavening out of baked goods or accidental breakage of eggs while gathering and we didn't want mom and dad to know — probably lots more, but those were the good ole' days.

Doris White
Waterloo, Iowa

Outhouse Concealed Evidence

Some outhouses had fancy lids cut to cover the holes. Some used a piece of board for a cover, and others used nothing and gave the flies immediate access. The holes varied with individual tastes. Some had different sized holes in the same outhouse. For instance, a large sized hole or a smaller one for a more petite-sized person or child.

Nothing was so frightening to a child as to enter a strange outhouse where the holes were cut extra large and the pit appeared extra dark and extra deep. I can recall perching on the edge of the hole, hands gripping the ledge on the seat board so hard that the knuckles stood out white and thinking, "Oh, my gosh! What'll I do if I fall in?"

The outhouse was used to get rid of things other than human waste, too. Many young boys did their first experimenting with smoking there and concealed the evidence by tossing it down the hole. More than one time, the alarm was given that the toilet was on fire and then it turned out to be a young lad with an ample supply of cornsilks. Before smoking in public became accepted for women, the outhouse was used for a smoking salon and down the hole went the circumstantial clues.

Wayne Cassel
Fowler, Indiana

Suckered Siblings

Back in the 30's we lived on a farm. One of my older brothers, who was visiting us, went out to the outhouse. Somehow he knocked his glasses case, with the glasses inside, down the other hole. He offered my younger brother and I a dollar if we got them out. I held a lantern down one hole while brother used a garden hoe. He was able to get the case on the hoe and bring it out. We cleaned up the case and gave it to the older brother. He took out his glasses, threw away the case and said, "Thanks suckers." When we complained to mother she said he was our brother and he didn't have to pay. If this is printed it will be the only money I got.

Mrs. Leonard Risker
Kansas City, Kansas

Putting Up Hay

Sure I remember the old outhouse with its Sears Roebuck catalog, and the times I nearly froze to death in the winter or the times I kept a wary eye on a wasp in the summer.

At that time, no one had heard of a hay baler. All the hay was put up "loose" and either rope slings or a hay fork was used to get it into the haymow. The hay racks all had sides, and in the center front was a "standard" to help hold the hay, and on occasion to wrap the harness reins around.

A neighbor had one end of the clothesline fastened to the outside of the outhouse. The hired man drove the horses and rack through beside it and the standard caught the wire — and the building went over. That wouldn't have been so bad except that a teenage daughter was "using the facility." At that point in the tale, everyone dissolved into such gales of laughter that I can't remember ever hearing how she was rescued.

How times have changed, and aren't we GLAD!

Mrs. Thomas Butcher
Rockwell, Iowa

Hit And Run

We lived in the country, and mother had just learned to drive the car. She was a little nervous about driving the first time, but this was the day she was going to do it. She backed the car from its parking place right smack into the outhouse, knocking it from its foundation. Of course it got to be a family joke, but my poor mother, with her wounded pride, never found it funny.

Bernice Manly
Arkansas City, Kansas

Under Pressure

Back in the 30's nearly everyone had a back-house. We lived in a small town in Missouri and I did housework for a lady. They had a two-seater outhouse that faced the main street. A friend of the woman came from California to visit for a few weeks. One day they both went to the toilet, and I was dusting at the time. Shortly I heard a big racket and I looked to see what happened. All I could see was their legs and heads sticking up. Their combined weight was around 350 pounds, so I guess that was too much for the board. It broke right down the middle, so quick they couldn't get off, and when their legs flew up they bumped the door causing it to fly open. It was the funniest sight I ever saw and when I could keep my face straight I ran out to help them. After things had quieted down I went into the room where they were. One look and we all got hysterical!

Name Withheld
Trenton, Missouri

A Front Row Seat

A friend tells me I must send in my outhouse story. So here goes. When I was nine or ten years old, the bull boosted my brother over the fence. He was carrying a bucket of milk in each hand. This made my two older brothers unhappy with that animal, believe me. So they proceeded to harness him and hook him up to a turning plow. I ran to the outhouse to view all this out the "moon windows." The outhouse was very near the field

60

they were going to plow. Mr. Bull was more than the boys could hold and he was soon dragging the plow wherever he pleased. Wouldn't you know he caught the corner of the outhouse, turning it over. My, how scared I was. Unhurt, but I decided that wasn't the best place to view the show!

Name Withheld
Strafford, Missouri

Slip Sliding Away

The time I laughed the most was the time my older brother used the outhouse at a friend's home.

He just got sat down and all but the seat fell apart and slid down a hill. The look on his face made everyone roar. He was there to impress a girl and he sure got the job done.

Mrs. Melvin Sampson
Akron, Colorado

Treading On Shaky Ground

During the course of the evening we womenfolks had to go to the outhouse. My sister-in-law and mother-in-law went inside and I was going to wait outside. It was cold and they told me to come inside, and as I stepped in the floor gave way and down we went, all three.

Now how to get out? We finally got my sister-in-law out and she went to get help from the men.

What a mess we were, we were fortunate that the weather was cold and nobody was hurt. But I'll never forget the time that we fell in the hole.

Mrs. E. Rewerts
Doniphan, Nebraska

Great Balls Of Fire

The outhouse was a place to take the catalogs. We had one about fifty yards from the house. We made some quick trips in the winter time.

One summer during a rain storm, the lightning struck the

outhouse. A big red ball of fire came down out of the sky and went in the front door and we had to make a new outhouse.

Nathan Corder
Kansas City, Missouri

"Not In Kansas Anymore"

I was too young to remember this tornado that struck our neighbors place a few miles from where we lived, but I have heard this story many times. It lifted the outhouse up and carried it about a half mile and sat it down in a field. All the time the hired man was inside, scared but not hurt.

Ellen Nelson
Hudson, Illinois

Not The Holiday Inn

I thought I was going to have to spend the night in the outhouse, and I didn't have my pillow or toothbrush, or any room service or telephone.

Our outhouse was far enough away from the house that no one could hear my calls when I got locked in.

Our four-year-old, unbeknownst to me, had snuck up and turned the board that we had nailed on for a lock. I yelled and kicked and shoved, all to no avail. I couldn't believe I couldn't get out of this predicament until someone missed me and came to my rescue.

At last my husband came outside, and I had climbed up on the seat and was wiggling my finger thru the half moon and yelling, trying to get his attention. He thought it was hilariously funny, and I did, too, after I got out. But I still didn't want to make any future reservations.

Dorothy Cochran
Bland, Missouri

Dolly Down Under

I was four-years-old when the Armistice was signed. I remember being frightened when the whistles and horns blew.

Before that all our visitors and the family talked about how awful the Germans were. My mother scrubbed the kitchen for a neighbor woman who was unable to do it herself, she had no money so gave my mother gifts she'd brought from Germany. She gave my mother a doll, it had real hair and a kidskin body, and it was to be for me. I didn't want anything that came from Germany, so I threw it in the outside privy — just think what it would be worth today!

Aleatha Kinney
Waterloo, Wisconsin

Outhouse Assault

We stopped at a cemetery near a small town in South Dakota to visit relative's graves.

An outhouse was on the premises, so I decided to look inside. As I went to step in, I stepped in a hole, and as I did I hit my head on the corner of the over-hanging roof. As I got to the car, I found that the cut was bleeding profusely.

Needless to say, I got a 30-mile lecture on the necessity of seeing a doctor. To this day, I hear about the day I got assaulted by an outhouse!

Madonna Storla
Postville, Iowa

Getting In The Groove

A few years ago my husband and I and two of our teenage daughters decided to take a trip to the Black Hills of South Dakota.

Since we had been there twice before, we wanted to take a different road or trail that was scenic. We drove for many miles through valleys and gullies, amongst the beautiful pines, and it wasn't a road that was traveled too much. As we drove along we came upon a gas station that looked as though it had seen better days, but our gas tank was getting low so we stopped to refuel. When I asked the attendant if I could use the restroom, he informed me there was none inside but there was one "up yonder" on the hill.

It seemed a long ways up there, but as nature was calling I decided it was now or never. The girls and my husband said they would wait in the car, so I reluctantly trudged up the incline to what looked like a dilapidated old shack, tipped to one side. I hesitated, but there were only two choices, either enter or take to the bushes.

The day was real sultry, and as I pushed the creaky door shut I didn't realize it had fallen down into a crevice on the floor. The inside was as dark as a sack of black cats, and none-the-less hot and stuffy.

As I got ready to leave, I tugged and pulled with all my strength, but it didn't budge an inch. By this time I was getting frantic and I imagined lizards and rattlesnakes all around me. I discovered a hole in the door where the door knob used to be, so I lowered myself and peeped through the hole and happened to see a man and his little boy walking by in the distance, evidently going to the mens' restroom "up younder."

I yelled at the top of my voice and asked him if he would please come and help get me out of there. He didn't hear me so I yelled twice more. He stopped and looked around, wondering where the voice came from. He finally must have gotten the drift so he came over and discovered what the problem was. He lifted the door up out of the groove and stepped back. I thanked him several times and he didn't say a word, but just walked away smiling to himself with a big grin on his face.

I often wondered what kind of a tale he told his wife when he got back to his car about how he helped a lady out of the privy.

When I got back to our car I found them enjoying a bottle of pop and munching candy bars. Seeing this I was quite irritated, remarking that the least they could have done was to come looking for me since I was gone a long time before returning. My husband replied, "Oh, I thought you fell in."

Mrs. William Urben
Worthing, South Dakota

Privy Gets Prized Possession

One day my mother was attending a P.T.A. meeting. As children will do when an adult is not around, things got out of hand. My brother brought his stilts in the house and was walking them by the dining table. The table was one of the old round tables with pedestal-type legs.

My brother lost his balance and over went the table, breaking my mother's prized possession, a little blue and white sugar bowl. This is where the fun ended. What would we do? Then one of us thought, throw the pieces in the old pit toilet!

Sorry I don't remember the outcome of our decision. But I am sure we didn't come out "scot free."

Lillie M. Haynes
Decatur, Texas

Blizzard Billet

The first year I taught rural school we had a big blizzard in November and I couldn't drive my car to school. A few days later my Dad took me there with a team and wagon and helped me make arrangements to stay at the home of a young couple near the school. I was made to feel quite comfortable even though there was no bathroom. Each evening before bedtime we'd take turns taking the flashlight and going to the outhouse by way of the cleared path.

One evening the husband came in from his trip with a strange look on his face. He finally had to admit he had accidentally let the lighted flashlight roll down in the hole beside him and it was at the bottom of the pit. We had to make our trips in the dark until they could get a new flashlight.

Mrs. Floyd Kauffman
Shickley, Nebraska

Ingenious Escape

We were entertaining our friends with a Sunday night supper. Our little daughter and her little friend, both aged five, excused themselves to go to the outhouse. It was almost dark. They were

65

gone for some time and a "blue norther" blew in with an awful force. The two little girls came running into the house as mad as wet hens, asking why we hadn't rescued them! It seems that the wind had blown the outhouse door shut, causing the wooden latch to fall into place, locking them inside. After yelling and screaming to no avail, our little daughter reassured her little friend that she would get them out safely. She started unrolling the toilet tissue from its holder, them took the cardboard cylinder, mashed it flat with her shoe, and slipped the flat cardboard through the crack in the door, unlocking it. We thought that was pretty smart thinking.

That was the only outhouse I've ever seen carpeted wall-to-wall in toilet tissue.

Our little girl has grown up and is the mother of twin boys, and is still using her ingenuity.

Mrs. Herbert Michalewicz
Rosebud, Texas

———————————■———————————

CHAPTER 6: Peek-A-Boo!

Peek-A-Boo!

About thirty-eight years ago we moved to a small farm in Arkansas. The "little brown shack" sat facing the highway. Our three-year-old son would go to the "potty" and leave the door open. I told him when cars passed the people could see him sitting there and he said, "No, they can't see me 'cause when I hear a car I shut my eyes."

Name Withheld
St. Francis, Kansas

Truth Or Dare

I was about nine years old when this occurred around 1911. I lived with my parents, sisters and brothers. We walked the mile and three quarters to our country school every day.

Our schoolhouse was built near the east end of the school lot. The boys' outhouse was built in the southwest corner of the acre lot and the girls' outhouse was built to the far northwest corner. For the boys to go near the girls' outhouse was a NO, NO. The girls were not allowed near the boys' toilet.

Well, one noon when the bell was about to ring for classes to resume, I made a dash for the toilet. Some of the pupils were already in the schoolroom.

Then I heard boys' voices right outside the little house. One boy was saying, "I bet you won't do it." "I dare you to" and "I bet you're afraid to." I sat on the seat scared and wondered what next when I heard, "Go ahead. Go ahead," and all the time the voices kept coming closer and closer. All at once the door was opening. I dashed into a corner holding up my pants. He came in, closed the door and quickly opened the door and was gone. The little house had no windows so it was dark on the inside and he never knew I was inside.

I was scared and shaking with fright and finally mustered up courage to return to the schoolroom, walked straight to my desk, never looking on either side. Nothing was ever said to me about this incident and I never told any one until several years ago, the boy that came inside and his wife celebrated their 50th wedding anniversary. They live in Texas. I sent them an anniversary card and enclosed a letter telling him about that incident. He said they and their friends had many laughs about it.

Mabel (Cron) Kirk
Griswold, Iowa

Bedtime's For the Birds

Just wanted to write to you about an experience I had as a child about an old outhouse. Seems after I got in bed every night I had to go to the outhouse. So, I guess my parents thought it was unnecessary every night as mom took me out before she put me to bed. Dad was a joker anyway and he thought up a joke to pull on me to break me of the nightly habit.

We had a three holer and the folks had an old empty bird cage sitting over one hole, so Dad tied a string to it. That night it was so dark and mom said, "Go by yourself."

I did, and about the time things were working for me, Dad pulled the string and the bird house fell over. I still don't know how I got to the house, but I jumped over the cage and went screaming to the house. Years later, Dad laughed and told me the trick they used to break me of going out ever night after I got in bed.

Fay Hammond
Cheney, Washington

Overexposed

The most embarrassing outhouse experience I had occurred when I was twelve years old. I was attending a little one-room rural school, where outhouses for boys and girls were discreetly erected some distance from each other, and also from the schoolhouse. It was during the noon recess. The students decided to play hide-and-seek. I had to pay a visit to the outhouse and my best friend, Louise, slipped in to hide in there. She watched through a crack while the boy who was "it" counted. When she saw her chance to get to base without getting caught, she flung the door wide and ran as fast as she could! Well, Louise happily made it to base without getting caught, but there I sat, on the throne, in full view of everybody. My skirt was not long enough to cover my bloomers, and I could not get up to close the door without exposing even more. All I could do was sit there, mortified, while all of the kids stared, and then went into hysterical fits of laughter. The girls doubled over from laughing so hard, and the boys rolled on the ground.

Finally, after what seemed like a century, Louise came back, slammed the door quickly, and beat a hasty retreat before I could get my clothes rearranged and take after her. I wonder why I was the only one who was not amused?

Eileen Grube
Gerald, Missouri

Hen-Pecked

Years ago usually everyone had one holers. One fellow decided he'd build a two holer. His neighbor wanted to be better so he built a three holer. One day he went in to use it and he had gotten to the third hole as the others were "well used." Suddenly he jumps out "with his pants down" yelling, "I've been bit by a snake, I've been bit by a snake!" not realizing an old setting hen had made her a nest in the third hole and as he sat down she pecked him.

Joe Linhart
Enid, Oklahoma

Jet Setter

Here is my story about the "little house out back." As we all know there weren't any "jets" during WWII. They came right after the war was over. One day I was sitting in our "little outhouse out back," my cares forgotten and deep in thought, when the first "jet" I had ever seen or heard came zooming over low and fast. I thought it was a bomb coming straight at me. I came out of the outhouse with my pants down. I think my hair was standing on end. We live on a farm and thank goodness no one was around to see me. My husband served two years on a Destroyer during WWII in the Pacific. I thought to myself, "I sorta know how they must of felt when they heard a bomb."

Katharine Hill
Smith Center, Kansas

Pigs Disturb Peace

When I was growing up on a Kansas farm about fifty years ago, outhouses were the going thing. Ours was a regular one seater with a Sears catalogue, but some were two seaters, with an actual roll of tissue and fancy cut-outs in the door.

Like us, our friend Vern had a small one out back. He also had a bunch of pigs that ran loose so they could forage for some of their food. The dog delighted in chasing those pigs all over the farm whenever Vern wasn't in sight. One day Vern was perched comfortably in his outhouse, bib overalls around his feet, when he heard that dog barking wildly and little pigs squealing with fear. He bolted out of there screaming some not-so-nice things at the dog as he tried to run with those overalls acting like hobbles.

Too late, he discovered the barking of the dogs and the squealing of the pigs was caused by guests who were standing by watching the whole scene with amazement.

Poor Vern had an even harder time trying to back into the outhouse. He never lived that down, but embarrassment must not damage a person's health, as Vern is in his eighties now.

Shirley Friedrich
Ephrata, Washington

Dances With Wolves

Outhouses were an institution in the twenties. We lived in the small town of Longton, Kansas. As usual my brother who was two years my senior "had to go" after darkness had set in. He was afraid to go out alone, so my mother insisted that I go with him and stand outside. I was afraid of the dark too, and as I stood outside in the darkness my imagination came to great fruition. My mother had washed some gray rugs that day and they were on the line drying. Wide-eyed I could see "gray wolves" coming closer as the wind waved them softly in the darkness. Not being able to constrain my fear further, I let out a scream and started for the house. My brother, unaware of my fears, but thought it was serious, came running (with pants down) and screaming too. We both fell into the arms of a frightened mother. That was a momentous night in my very young life.

Vera Close
Colorado Springs, Colorado

Top O' The Morning To You

This happened in the "good old days" of the outhouse - about 1925, when I was just a young married lady.

One morning I had to go to "the little house out back" shortly after sunup. It was chilly, so I left the door open so I could bask in the warm sunshine. I was thumbing through the Sears Roebuck catalog, which was a necessary accessory in the outhouse, when suddenly our neighbor from across the road was standing in front of the open door looking at me! I'm sure he was as startled and embarrassed as I was, but being a gentleman, he tipped his hat and said, "Good morning." I said "Good morning" and he went on his way. He kept some cattle in the pasture behind our place and had cut through our yard on his way to the pasture.

I never left the outhouse door open after that!

Myra Haferkamp
Independence, Missouri

Waves of Embarassment

The concussion from an enemy rocket of the nite before left our four holer intact except for roof and walls which were not in sight. This being MCB#5s and I as a member was using same when a train load of Vietnamese people went by, inside, on the roof, and hanging from the sides. No cover for me to run for after being caught with my pants down, so I waved, and folks, believe it or not, every man, woman and child waved back.

Ray Hooper
Sierra Vista, Arizona

The Wind-Blown Look

Many years ago, before graveled roads and running water in the house (some people might call it living in the sticks), I made the usual trip out to the little house (as we called it then), and had just pulled the door shut. Nobody would be by this road today as it was muddy, or so I thought. Well, a gust of wind blew the door open and there I sat with the catalog in my hands, when I heard somebody holler, "Hi —," he called me by my first name. After that the door was hooked. Was I ever embarrassed!

Mrs. Ben McKenzie
Laclede, Missouri

Musical Chairs

I was a freshman in high school and lived in a rural community. I came from a large family and my older brother Wilbert and I were especially close. The only time I'd used an inside toilet was at school and I just wasn't comfortable with it so I'd try to wait till I got home.

I lived about twenty miles from my school so by the time I got home, I was in a run. My daily routine (known by all my family members) was to run home, throw my books on the porch and run down to the outhouse. I could open the door, back in and pull my clothes down all at the same time without even looking.

One day I came running home, threw my books on the porch and continued my journey to the outhouse. When I sat down on

72

one of the "two-seater's" holes, I touched warm flesh. I wasted no time jumping up — forgetting what I had come to do. Wilbert was sitting on the same hole (fully dressed)! I was so embarrassed and humiliated I left in tears, but Wilbert was in tears from laughter. He thought it was quite funny. Now thirty years later it's a wonderful memory.

Shelby Gilmore-Morgan
St. Clair, Missouri

No More Night Trips

When I was a little girl, I lived with my parents in the last house out on the edge of town. Our nearest neighbor was a block and a half away. There was an empty field just south of our place where the town always had their fairs and carnivals. One night I woke up and had to go out to the little house. It was very dark and quiet. The carnival was all closed down, so out I went and sat on someone's lap. I started screaming and running to the house and my parents came running out. It seems some drunk had wandered over to our little house and fell asleep in there. I was sure scared and never went out there at night again.

Mary Alberts
Fremont, Nebraska

"Two Seats Here"

The subject of outhouses reminds me of the time that I had the "urge" pretty bad. Well, I rushed out to the little house out back and opened the door, which was not locked. My father-in-law was sitting there and it didn't bother him at all that I had opened the door. He just said, "Come on in, there's two seats here." Needless to say, I waited.

Juanita Buchholz
Peculiar, Missouri

Visiting Hours

My great-grandparents homesteaded the farm where I was raised and one of the neighbors down the road toward town had their outhouse close to the road they put through, in fact, it was facing the road. When the lady of the house was using the outhouse she would leave the door open and visit with the neighbors when they went by in their buggies. Someone asked her why she didn't shut the door and she said that way she didn't waste time visiting.

Mrs. Art Larson
Mauston, Wisconsin

The Preacher And The Privy

Do I remember "the little outhouse" or "the little outhouse out back?" I should say I do.

We lived near a small town and my parents were members of the Methodist Church there. The day I am referring to they were entertaining I think, two Methodist preachers, the regular preacher and another who was holding a meeting there.

My sister was younger than I and she wanted to go to "the little house out back," and wanted me to go with her. I didn't want to go but mother made me go with her.

This "little house out back" had some cracks in it and as we were walking down the walk I could tell this little outhouse was occupied, so I told her to come on and I walked on toward the hen house. I kept telling her to come but instead she went on to "the little house out back," opened the door and went in. I walked on to the hen house.

Later when we both went to the house I asked her why she didn't come on with me. She said, "I opened the door and he said, 'Shut the door,' so I just went on in, shut the door and set down." It turned out that it was our regular preacher at this nearby Methodist Church.

That happened many years ago as I am now eighty-two years young but will always remember about this very funny and embarrassing thing.

Mrs. Eugene Sharp
Mexico, Missouri

Frosty The Snowman

We had the movable privy out to the northwest of our house. This time was during a snowstorm with a good wind, and it blew the snow from the bottom side in back up the three hole. All this snow looked like a huge man over the hole. In one of the hurried trips in the nite to this house put a scare into us until we saw what it was.

Name Withheld
Denison, Iowa

A Picture Is Worth A Thousand Words

When my husband's ninety year old grandmother came to visit us, she went to the outside toilet. I was a person that put pictures in the toilet and I had a big man sitting above the hole and she went in looking up. She thought it was a real man and she quickly came out saying "excuse me," and came back to the house and told us she opened the door on a man.

My husband began to laugh and said, "Grandma that's just a picture." We all still laugh about it and this dear little grandmother lived to be ninety-eight years old.

Mrs. Clifford Cooper
Weeping Water, Nebraska

Raging Bull

The year before I was old enought to start to school, my brother, 16 months older than I, had just started to school. He started in first grade as they had no kindergarten in those days.

The day was a warm one in September. I had gone to the outhouse, which was about ten yards back of the washhouse. I had just completed my daily chore, and tore some soft paper out of the old Sears catalog, when I heard a noise in our yard. I looked out the door, my overalls still down to the floor. (As a pre-schooler, we wore only shirt and overalls. No underwear in the summer months and I was barefooted.)

Around the west side of our home came a big Gurnsey bull, running as fast as he could, because his owner, riding a horse, was right behind him. I darted in front of that rampaging bull, past the east corner of the washhouse, and on to the kitchen porch into the kitchen, still holding up my overalls and my bare little behind showing all the way.

Cecil M. Rodda
Osceola, Iowa

Of Mice And Men

When I was a small girl I will always remember the fright I had in the outhouse. I lost my mother at age eight, so I was left alone with two older brothers. At about nine years old a neighbor boy and my brother caught a mouse. They knew I was afraid of mice, so they came running after me. I ran for hiding every place I could find. Finally, thinking I would be safe in the outhouse, I ran to it, locking the door on the inside. Was in there quite some time when I decided to use it before going out again. Was settling down when over the top of the door came the mouse, right into my lap. I jumped up screaming, and ran out the door with my underdrawers down around my ankles. I kicked them and ran to the house crying. When our father came home and I told him, the boys got a whipping I don't think they ever forgot. I am <u>still</u> afraid of mice.

Edna Wheeldon
Stiller, Missouri

CHAPTER 7: Pranks On The Privy

Roller Derby

Outhouses and Halloween are almost synonymous. No outhouse was safe from the evils of the darkness on this notorious night. Every community had its own story of ol' Lady Smith making a late night call, and getting caught inside as the little demons of the night did their work tipping the little building over on its face as screams filtered through the cracks in the side.

One neighbor in our community solved this annual problem with great satisfaction. His problem was more oriented to the older pranksters rather than the "little" folk. During the afternoon, he jacked up his outhouse, inserted some planks underneath, and placed it on rollers. Just after dark, he went out and rolled it forward about four feet and retired to the house.

Needless to say, the next morning the little house stood stately erect. However, there was considerable evidence that persons unknown had made an attempt to do their dasterdly deed. While others were struggling to re-erect their outhouses, he easily rolled his little house back into place to serve its intended purpose.

Ivan Pfalser
Caney, Kansas

Bathing Beauty

We lived in the oil fields of Oklahoma and very few people had inside bathrooms. It was the custom for kids that age to push the outhouses over at Halloween. One boy's father decided to "turn the tables" on the kids' mischief. He moved the outhouse back a few feet. The boy, whose father had done this, was the first to arrive and eager to accomplish the feat. Of course it was dark and as he stepped into the disguised hole, he let out a yell that could be heard all over the community. His father had the last laugh, of course, as his aggressive son took a bath in a no. 3 wash tub.

Mrs. G.L. Baughn
Roseville, California

Dad Taken By Surprise

Every Halloween as far back as I can remember our outhouse was tipped over forward. So this particular Halloween Dad decided he was going to sit in it and find out who was doing this. He was hard of hearing and never heard anyone when — surprise! — he went over with the outhouse. By the time he recovered and got out, there was no one in sight. So he never knew who did it, but it never happened again.

Betty Miller
Chattaroy, Washington

A Sticky Situation

On Hallowe'en, many years ago, someone smeared sorghum molasses around the holes in our outhouse. Two neighbor boys got the blame, though we were never quite sure. It was a sticky mess with a few sticky bottoms until the "little house" was scrubbed clean with warm sudsy water.

Guinevere Koppler
Paris, Illinois

Muddled And Befuddled

Every year one could plan on the teenage boys going around to see how many outhouses they could turn over on Halloween. It was quite a chore at our house, we being only women, to right the building the next morning.

Two wires of the clothesline were fastened to one side of our outhouse. These needed to be undone before moving the building. One year the youngest sister decided to coat the ties of the clothesline with mud. After dark we heard the pranksters roaming around the outhouse. They they went on their way.

The next morning we quickly looked out wondering what we would find. The outhouse was sitting upright. They must have thought the mud just might be something else!

Mrs. A. Goossen
Okalona, Mississippi

Scared Stiff

My grandpa was the first and oldest cigar-maker in this particular town in Iowa. The store was located in front, the kitchen in the rear and the living room and bedrooms were on the second floor.

What I vividly remember is the story told to me by my "Old Maid" aunt about her recollections of a Halloween eve many years ago. She was making her final trip of the evening to the back of the house where the outhouse stood. In her hand she held the flashlight, and when she opened the door her light outlined the figure of the seven-foot-tall wooden Indian who, with cigars tightly clenched in his fist, stood grinning at her. (He normally was found in front of the building.) Needless to say, she forgot what she came to do and ran screaming back into the house.

Ginny Spechtenhauser
Gold Hill, Oregon

Mannequin Shenanigans

When I was a child, the favorite Halloween prank was shoving over outhouses. Having this happen a few times, my mother devised a plan to outwit the boys.

With we children helping, mother hung a pair of father's huge overalls in the doorway of the outhouse. We crumpled up old papers and stuffed the overalls. Adding a stuffed shirt and an old felt hat, it truly looked like a huge man standing in the doorway of the privy.

Sure enough, after all the lights were out in the house the pranksters sneaked across the back yard to the outhouse. Watching from an open window in the house, mother said she really enjoyed the commotion as the boys nearly knocked each other down as they fled from the man in the outhouse.

Mrs. Sterling Johnson
Holdrege, Nebraska

Going Out With A Bang

On Halloween eve, seven of us older kids, who with the neighbors had gone to our uncle's and grandparents' to pull some tricks, were returning home. In the distance we heard a loud blast, and in only a minute or two the second blast came from our outhouse and another went off in a few minutes more in another direction. While we were gone, someone had put dynamite in the outhouse. The other two were wired to go in unison. They found the men who did it. But the worst was our mother had just been there a few minutes ago.

Helen Glathar
Humbolt, Nebraska

From Monstrosity to Modern

On this Halloween I watched as my nephews sneaked and hurried through the tall grasses and weeds behind the plum orchard and scurried across the cow pasture in the moonlight. Minutes later I heard a crash as they tipped the outhouse.

The next morning I had a feeling of elation as I looked at the decayed monstrosity lying there broken into a thousand pieces of rotted lumber. I did not tell my husband that I knew the culprits, nor did I tell the culprits that I knew who they were.

It is true that we reverted to the old chamber pot over the winter, but in the spring we went modern!

Geneva Wynkoop
Shevlin, Minnesota

Night Deposit

One time our local banker came downtown the next day after Halloween and found an outhouse on top of his bank. That must have taken work to get that up there. And the banker had to get it off his roof.

M.F. Anderson
Polk, Nebraska

"Little Houses On The Prairie"

It was the morning after Halloween in 1936, and I remember well the two-holer outhouse where it so proudly sat right out there in the middle of the intersection of Main and Chautauqua Streets in downtown Chautauqua, Kansas. It was surely a dedicated group of boys that moved the building there. And no matter that its location made the old backyard bungalow handy for early morning shoppers, the cashier of Chautauqua State Bank found reason to frown when he discovered the contraption out front of his financial institution that morning. Come to think of it, the owner of the outhouse also found its location somewhat unhandy for those living at his address.

Although I was a country boy, I still recall when each home in my old home town of Wayside, Kansas, had its "little house on the prairie" proudly setting out by the alley back of the big house, and each business in the village had its own important little building out on the back lot.

Glen Defenbaugh
Independence, Kansas

Out-Housebroken

One of the most unusual outhouse stories I ever heard happened to my grandmother. When she was a school girl in rural northern Michigan, one of the older boys often sprayed the girls (with urine) through a knothole in the girls' outhouse. That is, until my grandmother hit his sprayer with a stick!

Amy I. Taylor
Springport, Michigan

81

Dogged By The Doghouse

I vividly remember the day my younger brother got angry because I was occupying the "necessary" building when he wanted to use it. What did he do? He pulled the doghouse in front of the door, took the clothes prop and riled up the nearby hornets' nest.

Talk about walking into a hornets' nest — I literally did! While trying to scamper over that doghouse I was stung four times in the hand.

To this day I give a hornet all the space he needs.

Wilma D. Barnes
Plainfield, Illinois

Got Superintendent's Goat

About 46 years ago, when I was a high school student, I arrived at the school building one morning to find an outhouse sitting inside the hallway. Inside the outhouse was a goat tied firmly to the door. There was a lot of giggling and wondering who would dare do such a trick. The Superintendent came and looked the outhouse over and smiled. Then he asked some of the older boys to help pull it outside.

Betty Jo Rexius
Lyman, Nebraska

He Could Not Tell A Lie

The story I remembered these last 57 or so years was told to my grandpa and me by a man who did odd jobs for grandpa around his furniture store. The man had his outhouse built on a small boat dock along a river in Missouri. He often tied his boat to the dock and made use of the outhouse.

One day some boys sneaked up and dumped it in the river. He asked his son if he had anything to do with dumping it. He wouldn't admit it so the man told him about George Washington and how he told his father he cut down the cherry tree and his father was so happy he told the truth he didn't punish him. He said, "Now I'll ask you again. Did you help dump my outhouse?"

And the boy said, "Yes, Dad, I helped."

His Dad then gave him a whipping, and while the boy was crying he said, "But Dad, I told you the truth like George Washington told his father. Only you whipped me."

The man told his son he didn't thrash him for telling the truth, but the difference he got whipped for was that George Washington's father wasn't setting in the cherry tree when he chopped it down.

I asked Grandpa if that was the truth and he said Will lived close to the river and he did have a little boat dock and there was an outhouse on it.

Name Withheld
Baldwin Park, California -

Ring Around the Collar

The outhouse incident that still brings a chuckle in our family happened when my daughter was four years old. She had been scolded by her grandmother, so to get even the child went outside and found the can of blue paint they had been using. She took the paint and brush to the outhouse and decorated the seat.

Very shortly thereafter, Grandmother and Aunty made a trip out back and stepped into the dark place. Just in time, Grandma smelled paint and yelled, "Hold everything!"

No, it wouldn't have been "ring around the collar!"

Marcie Sager
Mesa, Arizona

Look Before You Leap

About 55 years ago my aged Uncle Ed told of a late 1870s prank. A man annoyed by young boys knocking at his kitchen door would chase them first by running down the steps. He began running and leaping from his porch to gain better time. Some big boys waited until he was home and carried his outhouse and set it barely balanced on his porch floor, being as he had no roof over the porch.

The outhouse door had a screen door spring so they propped

the door wide open in line with the kitchen door. A boy rapped on the man's kitchen door and the man ran so fast out of his door that he bumbled into the outhouse, which fell over. The door banged shut, and the outhouse dropped on the ground on top of the door with the man inside. The man's wife and three big daughters rocked the outhouse over so he emerged in a rage. The man had the police come, he blamed Uncle Ed, who told me that he was too little. He also said he never saw a man so mad.

Emmett Kirby
Champaign, Illinois

Unwelcome Suitor

One farmer in the community was the proud owner of a new two-hole outhouse, complete with inside and outside latches. This farmer had a beautiful daughter who was being courted by a young man not liked or trusted by the family.

One day when the young man was supposed to call, the mother purposely went to the outhouse with the daughter, and upon leaving fastened the outside latch.

When the young man came he was told that the daughter had stepped out. He was told to wait if he so desired.

After two hours of waiting the young man left and that was the end of the courtship!

Mrs. Emil F. Plevan
Burnet, Texas

Crossed Wires

Two years after Mother died, Dad married a widow with three young boys, increasing our family to ten. Out of necessity an outhouse had to be built out near the chickenhouse. My step-brother Lee was thirteen and he thought it was great to tease his new "sisters" and he made our life miserable. He found an old battery and dreamed up an idea of wiring the outhouse to give us a shock, so every time he saw one of the girls heading that way he would scurry around back of the chickenhouse and touch the wires together. We kept complaining to our stepmother, who said we were just making it up — he wouldn't do that.

But one day as she headed that way, one of my brothers ran around and said, "Lee, I just saw one of the girls headed for the outhouse, what do you think?" He rushed out and connected the wires, then we heard a loud screech, the door flew open and our stepmother came flying out and around the back after Lee. He got a good tanning and the rest of us got a good laugh.

Audria Collins
Madras, Oregon

Wired For Sound

A young veteran, upon returning home from the service, set up a service station in the desert. No plumbing, so an outhouse was out back. A customer who had him working on a tire asked him what was behind, especially since women were hurriedly coming out and cars driving off.

The attendant laughed. "I get bored out here, and since I was in the radio corps I hooked up a speaker on the under-side of the board with several holes. When someone has been in there long enough to get comfortable, I take my speaker and say, 'I'm sorry, madam, but could you move over? I'm painting down here.'"

Mrs. Gus Krienke
Enid, Oklahoma

Devious Dad

On occasion, our dad would slip out, rake the back and sides of the outhouse with a stick and be back in the house before we mustered the courage to open the door and outrun what we knew was a wild animal trying to get in.

Betty Clayton
Mullinville, Kansas

Early Fourth of July

My husband said he used to wait until his older sister would get in the little house and then he would start throwing firecrackers up against the building. He said she would really come out of there. He says he got a lot of spankings over this, but he never stopped doing it as it was too much fun.

Betty Albright
Kingman, Kansas

Jailhouse Rock

Once the "big boys" at school created a game they called "Jail House." They caught the girls, and after much screaming, kicking and tugging, forced them into the coalhouse "jail," locked the door, and left them to sit amidst piles of coal until the bell rang for study time again.

The girls, disgusted with such a game, decided that their privey, which the boys dared not enter, was a good place of refuge. The very moment dismissal time arrived, the girls all fled to their wonderful hide-out to stay there in safety. The ingenious captors would then hasten to the water well and vigorously pump big buckets of water, then would hasten to dash the water high up through the half-moon holes, hoping to flush out the refugees. The girls crowded closely together directly under the stream of water and so remained "high and dry" as they all screamed in hilarious laughter.

After what seemed like ages of such activity, a girl's mother sent the teacher a note complaining that her daughter's dresses were simply loaded with coal dust that could not be removed even with hard washing in lye soap. The mother asked the teacher to please excuse her daughter from the game of "Jail House," as she could not afford to replace the dresses with new ones. All the girls were very grateful to that mother, as she caused an abrupt ending to the episodes.

Ah, yes, that grand old building, the privey, is gone with that era of life, but laughter and understanding of human nature was quite the same then as now, and ever shall be.

Daisy Brown
Prairie Village, Kansas

A Hard Nut To Crack

On this one particular day, my sister went to the outhouse after the noon meal and after the children were in bed. She was about ready to get out, when crack — crack — crack, something had hit the tin roof that sounded like stones.

To her delight she got the scream bit back that had welled up in her throat, and thought it was probably her husband that threw them on the roof on his way out to the barn. She decided she would trick him too, and went out to the barn and asked innocently, "Could you disk the garden soon?"

He said, "Oh, maybe I'll find time soon. Why do you want the garden disked?"

"Well, just a little bit ago," she said, "when I was in the outhouse, that walnut tree that is right beside it dropped some walnuts on the roof, so I just thought it would be nicer to pick them up if the garden was disked. That is right close by the tree so I would not have to pick the walnuts out of the weeds."

She saw that he was having a hard time keeping a sober face, but he answered, "Oh, yes, of course, just the next chance I get I'll disk it."

She turned to go into the house.

"Annie!" he called with a big smile. "That wasn't walnuts that you heard on the roof!"

She yelled back, "I knew it!"

Raymond T. East
Mt. Victory, Ohio

The Traveling Three-Holer

After two weeks of vacation we were now nearing our destination — home. We had been reminiscing the joys of the past two weeks, but now thoughts of home were rapidly replacing all other considerations. My husband, Dick, was concerned about the height of the grass and getting the paper started again. Becky was already at the window to catch sight of her friends. Debra had put away her book and was making comments about the neighborhood. I had thoughts of getting a pile of clothes into the washer and replenishing the refrigerator.

"Well, everything looks about the — " That comment was never finished because all talking stopped as the old Ford turned up the driveway. Four voices shouted at once, "WHAT IS IT?" "Beats me," said my husband. All I could say was, "I can't believe it." Sitting at the end of our driveway was a building. A building which certainly had not been there when we left two weeks ago.

Four doors flew open and we piled out, trying to comprehend this strange addition to our residence. Had we looked around, we would have seen many a face peeking out from behind the curtains with expressions of deep enjoyment and some displaying uncontrollable laughter. Finally, we cautiously opened the door of this latest addition. You guessed it, it was the largest 3-holer we had ever seen. It came equipped with a bushel of cobs and its own Sears Roebuck catalog. Yes, our good neighbors had pulled off another good joke on the Smiths.

Needless to say, the traffic increased on our street for the next few days. Everyone wanted to see this item from out of the past.

That night, as we started going through the pile of newspapers which had arrived while we were gone, we again discovered the three-holer. There on the front page was our front yard, and the center of the attraction was the three-holer. The headline read, "OUTHOUSE MYSTERIOUSLY APPEARS AT SMITH RESIDENCE."

As each day went by, my husband became more concerned about how to be rid of this house of convenience, which was not located in a convenient area. Meanwhile, it continued to be a topic of conversation as daily sightseers would stop and visit about the past glory of this item. Some young visitors had never seen this type of personal comfort house, and oldsters had many a story to share which started, "Why, I remember..." Yes, our three-holer was rapidly coming into its second glory. Many a visitor would open the door and let out a yell, "Hey, it's a three-holer!" The Three Bears who lived in the woods had nothing on this three-holer that was out of the woods. One hole for Papa's bare, one for Mama's bare, and one for Baby's bare.

We were having a lengthy discussion on how to get rid of our unwanted guest and get back a driveway, when yet another car stopped. My husband looked at me and I said, "No, it's your turn."

"Does this belong to you?" said a gentleman as he indicated the outhouse.

"It's on my property," Dick replied.

"How much would you take for it?"

Words my husband never thought he would hear. Words the pranksters never dreamed would be said. A very inexpensive deal was made. My husband could hardly wait to tell the supposedly unknown guilty parties that he had SOLD the three-holer. Later, one member of the guilty ones was heard to say (much to my husband's joy), "We paid $15 to get that moved to Dick's place and wouldn't you know, Dick makes money on it."

Sunday, what a pleasant surprise, we drove home from church and had our driveway back. The three-holer was gone. However, the next-door-neighbor stuck his head out his window and said, "Dick, someone stole your outhouse, but don't worry, we got the license plate and called the police so you will get it back."

Naomi E. Smith
Nevada, Iowa

Teacher And The Privy

My husband likes to tell about the time he went to the one-room school. The kids decided one day that they didn't want to go to school, so they waited til the teacher went into the privy (this was first thing in the morning so he still had his books and lunch pail in his hands). The kids took the clothesline down and wrapped it around the privy til the teacher couldn't get out. When it was time for school to let out, they went back and turned him loose. The kids were in a little bit of hot water for awhile.

Maxine Eastin
Yuma, Colorado

CHAPTER 8: Quips And Quotes

Mistaken Identity

We were having Thanksgiving dinner at our home, and there were between twelve and fifteen relatives present.

Our outside toilet was located near the alley.

In those days we used old catalogs for toilet paper. One of my brothers would go to the outhouse, sit, and look at the pictures in the catalog.

At this get-together I needed to make my appearance to the outhouse. When I got there the door was locked. At last I had to try again. The door was still locked. In thinking my brother was still in there I said, "Quit spending your time looking at that catalog. Other people need to use the toilet, so make it snappy and get out of there!"

In a very short time the door opened and out came, not my brother, but my cousin Ray. He was grinning from ear to ear.

Was I ever embarassed!

Edna Callison
Hannibal, Missouri

A Little Girl's Sacrifice

When I was growing up on the farm, we had an outhouse near a large grove of trees.

One particularly windy day Mother Nature was calling, so I headed for the little house. I got to the door and knew that the little building was not real sturdy. I had a fear that it would blow over with me in it. So I went into the grove and squatted down. There, a few feet away, I spotted a fifty-cent piece. I picked it up, took it back to the house, but knew I wouldn't tell anyone for fear of being teased.

Kids just didn't have their own pocket money in those days. So I took it to church the next Sunday and when the offering plate was passed, I slipped it in there. To this day no one has ever known about my "windfall."

Mrs. Ken Schweitzberger
Kingsley, Iowa

A Fond Farewell

Our Mr. and Mrs. Landlord from California had been supper guests in our rented farm home that evening. They always rented a motel room in town while visiting here, so, when a terrific rain storm came up during the evening and nine miles of muddy roads separated them from their beds, they had to remain overnight.

We did not have an indoor toilet, so before retiring, they had to take a flashlight trip on the muddy path to the relief station.

During breakfast the next morning, Mr. Landlord informed my husband to call a plumber and get a stool and septic tank installed pronto and take it out of his share of the crop.

That was the result of the nicest rain we ever had and a good goodbye to the two holer.

Mrs. Sanford Wickham
Holbrook, Nebraska

The Age Of Innocence

Back in the outhouse days, my sister-in-law and I were washing the noon dishes and looking out the window to see her six-year-old son and my five-year-old daughter peacefully sitting on the two holer out back. My sister-in-law and I decided it was time to have a little talk about privacy of boys and girls. When the children came to the house, I said to my daughter "that little girls didn't go to the toilet with little boys." She looked at me with very innocent blue eyes and said, "Oh, it's all right Mother, Calvin shut his eyes while I got on the seat and I shut mine while he did."

I'm afraid children today have lost a lot of their innocent look.

Trellabelle Pike
Macksville, Kansas

Dinner Is Served

Years ago Mother always exchanged help with our aunts at housecleaning time. It was our turn to have all at our house to do the housecleaning. Mother was busy making dinner. Everybody else was busy with their cleaning, washing, scrubbing, dusting, etc.

When dinner was ready, Mother said, "Everybody stop what you're doing and come to dinner." My brother, knowing one aunt had gone to the outhouse, hollered out to her, "Mother said you're supposed to stop right away what you're doing and come for dinner!"

Mrs. John Schmucker, Jr.
Medford, Wisconsin

"Hole"-Hearted Love

In 1920 I went to grade school at Arcadia, Kansas. The back outhouse was about 10 by 20 feet, a sixteen holer — eight for boys and eight for girls. One back served for both houses. The holes were back to back. When we had recess we all ran as fast as we could go, even if we had to go or not. The path was downhill. We had a new boy from Kansas City and a new girl in school, they were both in the fourth grade. This boy had a red cap and the girl had a new red purse. They both thought a lot of the cap and purse. As four boys hit the door the boy's cap got knocked off into one of the holes. The same thing happened to the little girl's purse! Both were looking with their heads partway in the hole on their side, trying to locate their belongings. Their eyes met, they fell in love, and I don't remember if they found the cap or purse. After high school they married. I have often thought, if they had grown to be very rich or important people, and someone asked the girl, "Where did you meet your husband?" She would probably simply say, "In the fourth grade."

Mrs. Daniel J. Strecker
Parsons, Kansas

Out of The Mouths of Babes

Although we had electric lights provided by a wind charger, we still didn't have plumbing. Our toilet was through a fenced yard about one-half a block in the meadow. There were four girls and no boys in our family at that time. This was very convenient for us because we were scared to go to the toilet after dark, so we always went together. For some reason it was too embarassing to say the word "toilet" in front of our dad, so we would spell it. When my little sister learned to talk she would say, "Who needs to go to the b-l-i-o-t?"

Joy Leazer
Crescent, Oklahoma

Riding the Rails

Back in the 50s, my folks needed a good outhouse. My father, who was a section worker on the railroad, was working near a depot which had been closed. The buildings were for sale, so Papa bought the sturdy outhouse. But how to get it home? Well, there was the motor car which ran on the rails. His co-workers helped load it up. Across the middle of Kansas they came, putt-putting down the track, yellow outhouse standing upright in the middle of the motor car. People along the way did a double take, bursting into laughter when they saw it. The men riding along beside it laughed and joked all the way in.

Virgie Hern
Altus, Oklahoma

Blushing Bride

When I first came out to the Midwest, I was a newlywed and had never seen or met my in-laws. As they soon found out, I blushed easily, so many jokes were saved for my presence! I had a time getting used to walking out and back to the "bathroom." I felt the whole little town was watching me coming and going.

One day when I was mustering enough courage to re-enter civilization, my husband's sister, who called me a city girl (and she was also full of the devil) asked me what took me so long out there. I knew I had to think fast or I'd be in the middle again so I answered, "I couldn't find the flusher!"

Veronica Clark
Sturgis, South Dakota

Kids Say The Darnedest Things

Our family attended a Fourth of July picnic held in a horse pasture, far from city conveniences. The men had set up an outhouse on the far side of the field. My three-year-old daughter had never visited an outhouse before and I had quite a time answering the question, "Mommy, where is the flush?"

Karin Hooks
Aiken, South Carolina

Sleepwalker

Our little house out back was quite a ways out back. Our second son often walked in his sleep, so I always listened for him to go out the back to make sure he locked the door again. He was about ten or eleven. One night he went out and I dozed, thinking he'd come back and it would wake me again. I got up, checked the door, locked it and went to sleep. About 6 a.m. someone banged on the back door. I grabbed my robe and rushed to the kitchen. Imagine my surprise when a tearful boy demanded, "Mother, why did you carry me out to that old toilet to sleep?"

N.R. Vair
Phillipsburg, Missouri

Old Habits Hard To Break

Nature's call to the "little house out back" may have started me on the road to reading, as my mother always told us kids to have a book or newspaper with us at all times to read while we were "doing our duty." So I did, and if there was nothing else handy there was always the old Sears catalog. Sometimes two of us sisters would go together to catch up with our news, to read and laugh. And no matter what we did, we always brought back a load of wood for the fireplace. "You're passing right by the wood pile," Mama would remind us, setting a habit that I follow even today. Oh, not that I have to go to the little house, but I do remember to take the trash as I go to water the wild birds, pick up the old newspapers to take them to their stack as I get up to start dinner, pick up the laundry for the washer as I get up in the morning to cook breakfast, things like that. It's a habit that help to keep my house tidy, saves a lot of steps and leaves me time to read, read, read to satisfy the other habit I learned from the outhouse.

Nell Womack Evans
Colorado Springs, Colorado

Potential Peepers

My brother was always making an outlandish "funny," so when a government game reserve was put in next to our farm with high towers built to watch for forest fires, his observation was, as usual, witty. He said, "Now there goes all of our privacy, they'll use those powerful binoculars to draw our toilet up close and then they will look through the cracks."

Mrs. Leonard Pitchford
Richmond, Missouri

Shiver Me Timbers

In 1959, the Amana Company of Amana, Iowa, was already famous for building good home freezers. That spring we attended the Tulip Festival at Pella, Iowa. One of the best floats in the parade was the one sponsored by the Amana Company.

On the beautifully decorated float was an old outhouse, with a big sign, IOWA'S FIRST HOME FREEZER!

Olivia Wiese
Davenport, Iowa

Best-Laid Plans Go Awry

I will never forget what happened on a cold, snowy, wintry night. It was about bedtime when I felt the urge to visit the "backhouse." I waited for awhile thinking the urge would go away, but it didn't, so I bundled up in a heavy coat, sock cap and overshoes. I took the flashlight so I could see to tramp a new path through the snow.

About six inches of snow had drifted in around the hole. After I had cleared the snow from around the hole, I sat down on the cold, wet hole. Guess what? The urge left me completely.

Verla Harmon
Russell, Kansas

Spotty And The Potty

One day we couldn't find my little brother and were becoming quite concerned, for he was quite small and must surely be lost. We feared he had wandered off into the woods, following his little dog "Spotty," who was always with him.

Finally after calling for Jerry and no answer, we started to call the dog.

Sure enough we heard whining and scratching from the outhouse, and there was "Spotty" and little Jerry, asleep on the "potty."

Mrs. Dorothy Cochran
Bland, Missouri

Outhouse Revival

During the Depression one of our neighbors was a very religious man with a large family. I am sure neither the man nor his wife could read, but they tried very hard to live by the word of God.

For instance, when he heard "Make a joyful noise unto the Lord," he insisted he and his family should sing or whistle when awake and not praying.

This poor man had no job and was unable to even feed his family alone. But he was happy and usually whistling.

Then he heard, "Go into your closet and pray." Having always called his "little house out back" the closet, he began to round up his family several times a day and crowd them into the "little house" (closet) to pray. To get them all in the closet was an art. First he gave each of his smaller children to his wife and older children. The wife and oldest daughter sat (to prevent the other children who were standing on the seat around them from falling through) then he wedged them in and finally he managed to tug the door shut. And they all prayed aloud.

The last thing they did before going to bed (they slept in their clothes) was go into the closet and pray. This whole scene being repeated several times a day became too much for the rowdy teenager who lived a few doors from them.

Some way the teenager had managed to own a beautiful well-working cow pony, from which he had taught himself to rope almost anything at first throw and full running speed.

One beautiful moonlit night as the "closet prayer meeting" was in session the teenager rode past at full speed, something he seldom did unless he was sure all the children were inside, and roped the little house, yanking it over backward off its location and most of the length of the garden behind it. Miraculously no one was hurt! But that put a stop to the closet prayer meeting for which the children, and I am sure the wife, were very happy.

Della May Clifford
Garber, Oklahoma

Construction Zone

The topic of outhouses came up just when my husband and his step-brother were in the process of building what my husband calls "the little house on the prairie."

We live in the country, a half mile off the main road. The men share a workshop a little ways from the house and decided the "little house" was a necessary item.

My husband, with his sense of humor, found an old window blind and painted a sign and posted it on the site. The sign read "The Future Site of The Little House on the Prairie, A and B

Construction Company." The A and B, being their initials. This was for the benefit of relatives coming for the weekend.

Bonnie Buzzard
Beecher City, Illinois

Headline News

When I was eight years old, I had to go to the outhouse. There was a dark cloud coming up in the west so I hurried to get out to it. Just as I was ready to go back to the house a terrible wind storm and hail started to come down. My first thought was to stay in and not get out in the storm but just that quick I said to myself, "I can't stay out here because if something happens to me, it will come out in the paper where I was." I returned to the house in the hail and wind.

Berneda Brown
Fairbury, Illinois

Outhouse Led A Charmed Life

Twenty-five years ago, we were lucky enough to build a new modern house. We were so proud of it all and especially the "bathroom." No more going out to the outhouse which stood in the corner with evergreen trees on the west and north. The years have gone by with the trees growing taller and taller and the outhouse standing unused over a quarter century. A wood shed and a utility shed were built in front of the outhouse which was eventually erased from memory and forgotten.

August the first of this year we had a terrible wind, rain and hail storm that did so much damage to field crops, buildings, trees, and everything in its path. We lost two barns, roofs off of other buildings, trees were uprooted and limbs broken off of other trees. Our satellite was destroyed by a neighbor's grain bin that was blown into our yard. It hit the garage house, satellite and then wound around a tree by the driveway.

Our daughter and her family came out a few days later to see all the damage done on the farm. As we looked the farm over seeing all the destruction, our ten-year-old granddaughter looked at me and said, "Grandma, how about the outhouse?" I said, "I never thought about it. We'll have to look." As we came back to the house we looked behind the wood and utility sheds and there nestled in the corner protected by the grown trees, in all its glory and not a scratch on it stood "Mr. Outhouse."

Mrs. Raymond Bauer
Iola, Kansas

A Happy Ending

In German an outhouse was called a "backhouse." Each farm had one and a fancy one had three holes.

We have one in our yard with two holes. A half moon on the east wall. There is still a Sears Roebuck catalog in a box there.

When our three children were little, our daughter wanted me to go with her with the flashlight at night. Usually it was when I was washing dishes. The howling coyotes would frighten her. Sometimes we had to sweep snow off the seat board.

But when I was home with my folks in South Dakota my dad built a toilet and cob shed under one roof.

My one sister went to live with her boyfriend during the week-end and stayed all night. My parents did not approve of this! So my other older sister took her shoes and hid them in the cobs, thinking she would have to stay home then. But time and again she would go again on Saturdays and bake for him.

After two years of teaching she announced that they were married all this time!

Esther Herman
Riverton, Nebraska

Squeaky Wheel Gets The Grease

The golden days of yore weren't all that golden, especially when the temperature dropped to zero or below.

The outhouse stood about forty feet from our house, and well do I remember the dark, windy night I got frightened out of my wits.

We had a windmill that screeched as it turned in the wind.

This particular night had been devoted to the young folks telling ghost stories. Then, for me, the "call" came. I persuaded an older sister to accompany me. We started out bravely enough.

Halfway down the hill, a gust of wind hit the windmill, and the horrible screeching started. Thoroughly frightened, I screamed and screamed. When at last I stopped for breath, I heard my sister say, "It's only the windmill." I finally calmed down enough so we could go on about our business.

This happened sixty-five years ago.

Mattie Murrain
Liberty, Missouri

Where There's Smoke There's Fire

This happened about fifty years ago. We lived on a farm and the four of us boys' ages ranged from fourteen to twenty years. One afternoon after dinner the four of us got done and we went to the outhouse. Dad watched us and said to Mother, "Just look, there are only two holes and all four got in."

He watched us from the windows, and soon said, "Mother, just look at this," and they saw the smoke coming out of the vent hole. But they didn't tell us about it until one Sunday. Dad pulled out a package of cigarettes after dinner and told us all we had to smoke a cigarrette in front of him and Mother.

Then is when he told all about this incident. We all had red faces, but before it was all over, we had one of the biggest laughs ever together.

Edgar Griess
Grand Island, Nebraska

No Loitering In The Privy

My Grandpa was fond of telling us kids stories of his childhood. It seemed to us he was always having a good time. We would eagerly anticipate each new story and kept egging him on to tell us more.

One day Grandma said, "Now I will tell you one you will really like." She told us Grandpa attended a country school and

100

there was a two-holer at that school. Some of the boys would wait until the teacher rang the bell to end the recess period then they would make a beeline to the two-holer. One day Grandpa was the last one to leave the outhouse. The teacher pointed a finger at him and said, "You stay after school." Grandma smiled slyly and left the room. Grandpa said, "Two hundred times I wrote, 'I loitered in the privy.' That took a long time. It was nearly dark when I finally got home but I never pulled that trick again, you can bet your sweet LIFE."

Mrs. Don Monthei
Jefferson, Iowa

Outhouse At The Office

My brother worked for the space program out in California. The energy crisis was extreme, with the price of gasoline on everyone's minds at this time.

He had a very stressful job helping to work out the problems of space flights, so when he was home on vacation, it was very peaceful here on the farm. I noticed him taking a picture back of our house.

I didn't know until several years later that he used the picture to ease the stress at work.

My brother Marlin made the annoucement, "I have a brother back in Iowa who has a gas generator energy system and I have a picture to prove it." He said, "The storage tank is in the center of the picture and the gas generator is in the background."

The men he worked with soon realized they were the victims of what used to be farmer's prank, when all they could see in the background was the old outhouse and propane tank that holds the gas to heat our house with.

Incidently, the old outhouse still stand in the same place today.

Donald Larsen
Burt, Iowa

The Santa Outhouse

My mother liked being surprised for Christmas, but she was

very good at guessing what Dad planned for her. The Christmas of 1933 Dad ordered a good solid outhouse made up for her at a hardware store.

He asked an uncle who had a truck to go for the two-seater of new pine early Christmas morning.

When the truck rolled in we all rushed to the door to look out.

My mother began to clap her hands but she was really surprised.

My husband and I live on the homeplace now and the Santa Outhouse is now a nice home for a banty hen and her chicks.

Evelyn Liggett
Edgewood, Illinois

Waterlogged

I thoroughly hated and destested the little house out back during the early years of our married life. The day we finally were connected to water and sewer, my neighbor lady said she was going to let the water run all day. I replied, "I'm going to flush the toilet all day."

Doris Benson
Montevideo, Minnesota

To The Victor Belongs The Spoils

The summer I was eight years old my father decided that we needed a new facility, so he set out to build one. He did all of his own carpenter work so it wasn't any chore for him. My brother, sister and I watched eagerly each day, all secretly planning how we would be the first to use the new structure.

The morning arrived when the building would be finished. That morning I arose with a raw scratchy throat and a head that felt as though it were filled with cement. Not wanting to lose out on my secret plan, I concealed how badly I felt and joined the others under the shade of a nearby tree. About the middle of the afternoon the project was finished, and when father had hung the door, and being a little disgusted with our bickering, he said, "Now, everybody run!"

Run we did, and I, being the most fleet of foot arrived first, went in and closed the door. But I had no more than got on the throne when I pitched headlong to the floor in a dead faint. I fell against the door so it took a little while to dislodge me. Father carried me to the house and put me to bed. The next morning I awoke with a 104 degree temperature and my whole body a firey pink from head to toe. I had a severe case of red measles and was a very sick child for several days. Believe me, that is one outhouse that is deeply etched in my memory.

Mrs. Lawrence Henry
Ellsworth, Kansas

Brothers' Invention

In the 1930s there were three brothers who were always thinking up things to invent. One day they decided to make a "wiper" for the outhouse. They got their mother's mop and wet it, then put a hole in the back of the outhouse and stuck it through. When they stepped on the end of the mop handle the wet mop flipped up under the hole.

They got it all ready, then got behind the outhouse to wait for their first victim. They heard someone coming, it was their mother. In she went. They waited. When they heard her tearing paper from the old catalogue, they stepped on the mop handle, and up came the wet mop, giving their mother a swat. She just about tore the outhouse down trying to get out. When their father got home and heard what had happened, the boys said they received the worst whipping they ever had. That was the end of their outhouse wiper.

Mrs. Vera Gleason
Beaver City, Nebraska

Pie-Eyed

My favorite story of the little house out back that I remember is about my sister and her pie.

My older sister, an older brother and I attended a rural school where all eight grades were accommodated.

The two little houses out back were situated a distance north of the schoolhouse, one to the west and one to the east.

It was customary in those days that these farm children who got up early and maybe walked to school, to eat a snack at recess that came at 10:30 a.m.

My sister couldn't resist the temptation of chocolate meringue pie in her lunch pail. Another girl in an upper grade started to tell her a ghost story as they were walking north to the little house out back. My sister was absorbed in the story and failed to eat much of her pie.

After they reached the inside of the little house, the climax of the story was reached with a scary ending. This caused my sister to jump and to drop her pie, meringue side down on the floor of the little house out back.

Needless to say, she did not get to eat her chocolate meringue pie that day after all.

Agnes Saunders
Wellington, Kansas

A Stranger Among Us

How well I remember the little house out back. I was four years old and one day I tried opening the door and it was locked. I yelled but no one answered. Momma came and still no answer. So we started to see who was accounted for. Everyone was there, so we decided it had to be a stranger and he didn't want us to know who it was. By the time our Dad came home we were pretty scared. He got the door open and there was no one in there. The hook had fallen down when the door was shut. Being so young they couldn't convince me that there hadn't been someone in there and they had sneaked out. That was in '42, and I married in '56. We moved into a house that had a little house out back. Well, you might have guessed, I had to make a late night call, and my husband had to go with me. We laughed about that many a time.

Beulah Payne
Bloomfield, Iowa

A Mystery Explained

Our outhouse was different than any other we ever saw as it had accommodations for two adults with a lower seat with a small hole, about six inches in diameter, for small children. In our kitchen we had a hand pump and sink which were lower than most so young children could wait on themselves. We raised all kinds of fruit which we canned for our own use. One year my mother was sick and we had peaches which needed to be canned and it was up to me to do it. I had a relative who offered to help me that had a little girl below school age that came with her. While we were doing the canning we noticed she was getting a drink of water then she would go outside,. She would soon be back and get another drink and go out again. After doing this several times her mother asked her why she was doing this. Her answer was that she was getting a drink so she could go out and sit on a nice little hole, then get another drink so she could go again.

Lucile Chapin
Appleton City, Missouri

Pit Stop

We were traveling from Kansas City to Sedalia, Mo., on a Sunday afternoon. Many of the stations were closed. It became very necessary for the little two-year-old to stop.

Finally dad decided an outside facility would do. It must have been pretty dark inside because our son made a request — "Daddy turn on the 'ite please." Of course there wasn't any light.

Mrs. Gene Wetzel
Walters, Oklahoma

Sisterly Advice

Although we are raising our family in times of modern bathrooms, I'd like to share an outhouse experience with you. My husband had taken our two eldest daughters (ages 6 and 8) on a weekend camping trip — complete with tents and outhouses. The girls waited as long as they could before they finally gave in to mother nature. The eight-year-old went in first, and on her way out, my husband heard her say to her little sister, "It's not too bad — if you don't look down!"

Sandy Lynn
Elmendorf A.F.B., AK

Conversation Piece

A snapshot of the outhouse was the picture left of the only building left on the home where I grew up. My son asked for pictures of any kind to hang in his office. I had the photo enlarged to 8 by 10, framed it and sent it to him. His employees liked it and he enjoyed the comments.

BMS
Council Grove, Kansas

City Slicker

Reminisce about outhouses, backhouses, the privy, etc., I sure can. I still have one here on the farm. The reactions of some people are great! I have a bathtub, sink, hot and cold running water, but no septic tank for stool.

When a 25-year-old young man came to spend a weekend, who had always lived in cities, he asked for the shower and I said there was just a tub. His look of utmost unbelief that anyone could live without a shower was funny, but the best was yet to come when "Where's the bathroom?" was asked. I said, "Take the flashlight and follow the path." I'm sure he thought he was back in medieval days. "Are there any skunks down there?" he asked. "I sure hope not," I answered. He bravely fared forth, very happy for the dog, who waited outside the door.

Then he asked the question about a bathroom during the night. I told him he needn't go way down there, "but go away from the house far enough that my flowers weren't molested."

He's been back several times, no questions asked, he just grabs the flashlight and says, "See ya later." Then, "What is Reader's Digest doing down there?" "To read, of course," I told him.

"READ!" he expostulated.

My answer, "A very nice place to read."
Another shocked look.

Beulah Carter
Sheldon, Wisconsin

Pennies From Heaven

It was April 28, 1909. My papa had that very day married my new mamma. The guests had all gone home. I needed to answer the call of nature so I went to "the little house out back." There, up overhead on a two-by-four, my fingers just happened to feel something move. To my great joy I had found two dimes, two nickles and a penny.

Today that wouldn't mean much to a eight-year-old child. To me at that time it was as good as an oil well today.

Christine Nofsinger
Oxford, Kansas

Hickory Smoke Rolls Out

When we were married over 50 years ago, we moved to a neglected farm. There was only one good building, the barn. The house was a disaster, no water or indoor facilities of any type.

At my urging my new husband began to construct an outhouse in the corner of the back yard. Before the seating arrangements were installed, the weather became very cold and butchering time was upon us. Since we had no smokehouse he decided it wouldn't ruin the new outhouse to smoke the meat in it.

Soon the hickory smoke was rolling out the backside of the outhouse. When a neighbor saw the smoke he thought it was so funny and told everyone.

We had a real problem living that one down. To this day, my husband is called Smoky by some of his friends.

Dorothy Miller
Knox City, Missouri

CHAPTER NINE: Ode to the Outhouse

Outdated Architecture

There was one on every farm,
A structure important as the barn,
Was used on cold days and warm.

Its dimensions were around 4' x 4',
Had a bench and one door,
With a catalog on the floor.

Now a memory obsession,
Not a modern Trivia question,
But what is it? Keep on guessin'.

Child of today says, "Even as many hints you give me,
I don't know but Granny told me positively,
That it's what oldies called an outdoor Privy."

Marjorie Andreas
Bayard, Nebraska

The One-Room Cottage

It was a little cottage
So very, very small,
It had no living or dining room

And no bedroom, kitchen or hall.

It was just a one-room cottage
Furnished with three seats but no desk,
It had a number of magazines and papers
And people went there to read and rest.

Some saw fit to go there
Where they could read and make wishes,
While glancing through Montgomery Ward
Or just to avoid doing the dishes.

The young ones went there to hide
If trouble was in the making
Any and all household chores to do
Or the yard needed raking.

One could hear giggling
If girls were there,
And boys were in the horse lot
With small rocks the cottage pelting.

That cottage was cold in the winter
And drafty as could be,
But not so in the summer
There under the big oak tree.

Such a tiny little cottage, furnished with
Two large seats and one very small,
And the main reason for going there
Was in answer to Nature's call.

> Gussie Stanfill Coatney
> Alma, Arkansas

The Little Shack Out Back
Oh how well I remember that shack

MY FOLKS BACK TO THE BASICS

Stood between the house and the barn out back.
Was a good place to hide when time to do dishes
With Wards and Sears catalogues we look through and made
wishes.

All summer until late in the fall
We watched for snakes, some years never saw any at all.
Papa had it bolted to posts,
He knew what happened on Halloween with all those ghosts.

Some were three holers and some had more
Once we had one was so big it had four.
Grandpa had padded one with fur, "Just for Grandma," he said,
We kids liked that one the best, we'd wait our turn, faces red.

A hook made of wire on the inside of the door
And of course it had a wooden floor.
On wash day it was scrubbed with hot wash water using a broom
We kids took turns doing this chore, and how we did fume.

Ladies that were really high toned would say,
"I'm going to Mrs. Jones," others called it the old Privy. (Webster's
says it means Private)
Now people take pictures of paint the few there are left
Some make them of cloth to hold toilet paper for a craft.

People talk of the GOOD OLD DAYS, how soon they forget
Yet I remember when the cat jumped from the rafters to the floor,
I was so scared that I went right through the door.
Papa had to put on hew hinges and a wire to hold it shut.

Mrs. George Wyant
Cook, Washington

Old Two-Holer
Many daydreams I recall,
Were spun in the outhouse

ODE TO THE OUTHOUSE

When I was small.

Mother would call
"Come do the dishes!"
Old Mother Nature, invariably
Would change her wishes.

To the old shanty
We would retreat,
Looking thru Sears & Roebuck
Was a real treat.

After what seemed like hours
We got back,
To find the dishes
Were all still stacked!

When the north wind blew
We would hurry
"Our throne" was neither
Padded nor furry.

Thru hail and sleet,
Rain and snow,
"Like the Mail —"
We had to go!

Name Withheld
Oketo, Kansas

Memories
Here is a gift most practical, it's true;
The pages are soft, we sometimes use two.
We know you'll find it most useful indeed,
Not only for softness, but interesting to read.

As the pages are torn in the backward direction,

You'll find by fall, it is the harness section.
That little house, you've often heard us say,
Is very cozy, and far out of the way.

As you sit there alone,
Quietly bowing your head
The book will please you
As the pages are read.

Now sitting on the seat so comfy, tho cold; would be very well, if
you'd not be too bold.

For sometimes you'll find the seat will pinch,
And your pleasure will end — that is a cinch!
>   Alice S. Caviness
>   Canon City, Colorado

Pondering Life
An old gray building sits forlorn
Off yonder by a field of corn,
With moon and stars its artly adorn.

The air is brisk on this frosty morn,
And goose bumps cover where pants were worn...

A page from Sears is quickly torn
As you sit and ponder why you were born!
>   Lois Thomas
>   Tulsa, Oklahoma

Little Outhouse On The Farm
There's a little house here on the farm
That's used by one and all.
It isn't much to look at, in fact it's very small.

It has no picture windows, no welcome on the door.

ODE TO THE OUTHOUSE

No heat inside to keep it warm,
No carpet on the floor.
There's only one seat in the house,
It's made of old oak lumber.
But still it serves its purpose well,
Been used by quite a number.

Everyone who visits me must go to see the place
And when small children want to go
Sometimes it's quite a race.

No matter what the weather be,
Sunshine, rain or snow
If you get the urge to see the place
Then down the path you go.
When nature gives her warning, as she does to every one,
We grab our coat no matter what
And down the path we run.

Down to the little house again, nestled among the trees,
Sometimes the wind is howling cold and you think you're gonna
freeze.

What is so popular about this house
Oh, surely you must know,
A little outhouse on the farm is a place we all must go.

L.L. Owen
Springfield, Missouri

INDEX

A

B

C

INDEX

INDEX

S

T

U

V

W